For you...
Yes you!!!

One cup of #joy, one pinch of #gratitude

PLANT-BASED LOVE STORIES

CHEF CYNTHIA LOUISE

GRATITUDE

[A love letter]

A Love Letter to My Body

Dear Body,

I appreciate you. I really do. And I promise
to show you more respect, more compassion,
and more love.

You are the only way I can experience the
reality and the beauty of life.

You of all things are deserving of my love,
not my criticism, and I promise to treat you
better as I navigate my busy life.

From
Me

Chef Cynthia Louise xx

P.S. With love, care and gratitude
to your incredible body

Food is a right not a privilege

Contents

Introduction

I'm a woman. A mum. A business owner, a best friend to my girlfriends and a lover. I'm passionate about food and soil and nourishing your body. I hate kale. I laugh out loud. I swear. A lot. I will sit cross-legged on the kitchen table and eat from a pot. I'm a chef.

I create damn good meals which nourish your organs with simple recipes that remove the confusion around food.

I'm not gluten-free or vegan but my spectacular girlfriends and man friends are (#bless them), and because I love them so much I want to make them beautiful meals in the way nature intended – and to get rid of all the bullshit that comes with diets and nutrition and the anxiety that comes with deciding what to eat.

Nature has figured out what is good for us.

I make food that is as natural and free of human interference as possible – and I have a great time doing it.

So here's a situation: some people hate cooking, but I'm all day in the kitchen with the music on, loving up on myself and spilling stuff, burning stuff and nailing the occasional recipe (my oven and me have a thing to sort out I'm telling you).

I'm not one of these neat, tidy, always-have-makeup-on women and I'm especially not the World's Greatest Chef, but I **love** food. I've learnt what feels good for my body and from that, knowing my whole life has changed as a result.

That's what I want to show you. How to make food that feels good for your body so you're not counting the calories and you're not clocking the carbohydrates and you can just forget all your rules and enjoy eating.

When you make one of my recipes – whether it's my Eggless Omelette, my Glazed Miso Pumpkin or some Coconut Yogurt Labneh Maple Frosting (yes you did read that accurately) – it **feels** good in your body. Your body isn't fighting it, it's loving it!

This is what I teach people at home, online, in my classes, and this is what I teach **myself** every day – how to cook with natural ingredients that can form a delicious Creamy Mushroom Pasta Sauce which makes you feel good. And without all the dairy and the crap sugar and the gluten.

Right now I live in Bali (#gratitude) and my girlfriends and my friends come around and eat my BBQ Pulled Smokey Shroom Burgers or some Vegan French Toast or my incredible "Spag Bowl" and it tastes good and it feels good and it **is** good – and then I watch their thoughts creep in.

"How many carbohydrates does this have?" and "is coconut milk bad for you?" and "won't I get fat if I eat this?" – and I'm like STF up.

Come back. Come back to how your body feels. You've just eaten a meal made with fresh, natural ingredients, and your body knows what to do with it because it's all connected to nature.

When I get people to feel how good this food is, everything changes.

Their bodies change. Their thoughts become kinder. Their energy changes.

I get email after email, message after message from men and women who have had the privilege of attending my workshops or taking my classes online and they can't believe the amount of weight they've lost. They're not doing some 12-week diet, they're not depriving themselves and they're not doing this complicated mental gymnastics every time they try to put something in their mouth, they're just eating real food.

That's what all of this is about.

When you start eating food that makes you feel good, your weight balances. Your mind calms down. Your skin clears up. Your thoughts become alkaline.

You stop beating yourself up over what you eat and you fall in love with cooking and eating again.

You fall in love with yourself.

There are two important things in this world:
1. You
2. You

If you've ever met me in person you know I swear. I don't care. I'm passionate. I love what I do. I love who I am and I'm unapologetic. I also laugh. A lot. Laughter brings a joyful state of feeling and it's these joyful states that I want to cultivate – especially while I'm cooking.

I'm also a certified Inner Critic with a Masters Degree in Body Shaming and Giving Myself A Hard Time. Here's another situation: one day I'm bloated – because sometimes that's just a fact of life when I have my period – but what was worse was this: my mind became bloated as well.

I was looking at my belly and going "Geez I'm bloated". So what do I do next? Well check out this pro move: I call my boyfriend (at the time) over and say "Look at me – aren't I bloated? I feel so fat".

Ever done something like this? Perhaps you've done **exactly** this.

And then I look at my thighs, because they're close to my belly, and I say "Gee, aren't they thick?". And my butt is next to my thighs so naturally I'm looking at my butt and saying more stupid things and before you know it my mind is bloated. Bloated with toxic thoughts about myself.

When I first noticed how I talk to myself I was shocked. As a woman I see that we do this to our selves. I'm sure men do it as well, and it's just so toxic.

There's only one thing more important to me than my health – only **one** thing – and that is my thoughts.

I had to change my focus and find all the things about my body that are A-mazing.

I look at my hands and I go "Wow! Without these little glories I couldn't cook and stir and touch and make love. They are fantastic".

Look at this face! Look at these beautiful lips and this incredible tongue with these thousands of tastebuds. Without them I can't nourish myself with food and flavour and delight. I can't breathe deeply and I can't whistle or kiss or swear at my burnt food and I can't laugh till I'm crying with my girlfriends.

These are the differences between acidic, inflammatory, dis-ease causing thoughts and alkaline, healing, health-creating thoughts.

What we need to do is put the Inner Critic to one side. Acknowledge her (thank you very much), allow her to be there (because she's never going away), and then turn **our attention elsewhere.**

We need to practice loving ourselves.

For me it starts with my thoughts. And when I'm thinking good thoughts I feel good emotions. When I feel good emotions I turn the music up in the kitchen which makes me feel even better, and I cook. I nourish my body as I'm nourishing my soul.

I feel good from the inside, which makes it even easier to love myself.

Cooking takes time – but so does being sick

I made spaghetti sauce the other week and all my friends were like "Jeez this is bloody good Cynth!".

CONFESSION: it was the same recipe as last time.

But guess what? That week I made some money. I went on an adventure. I hung out with friends. I had sex. I ate well.

All of those good feelings went into that sauce. That sauce created more good feelings and on it goes.

You can do the same in your life. That's where you and I are going to work together.

I won't bullshit you either. Cooking takes time. But so does being sick.

If you're a busy person (and let's face it EVERYBODY is – it's become like some stupid badge of honour) then just cook one or two meals a week. That's all. You'll have leftovers, so that's four meals. You're already winning. Just go from there.

The last thing I want to do is take a woman into a psychopathic state because "Chef Cynthia's recipes are so long...". Everyone can make these recipes. Even men (and you know that I love men).

You'll make meals for people who will say "Jeez that's bloody good" and they will have no idea that it's vegan. Or dairy free. Or whatever. They won't care and neither will you because it feels good, it's close to nature, and your body knows exactly what to do with it. End of story.

-Isms

I'm not into veganism. Or keto-ism. Or paleo-ism. Or any of your food-combining-6-week-planning-low-carbohydrating-isms.

But some of my recipes are vegan. Some of them are probably ketogenic. Or paleo.

They're all good for you though. They all make you feel good.

Here's the difference.

My mum always tells me to eat beans.

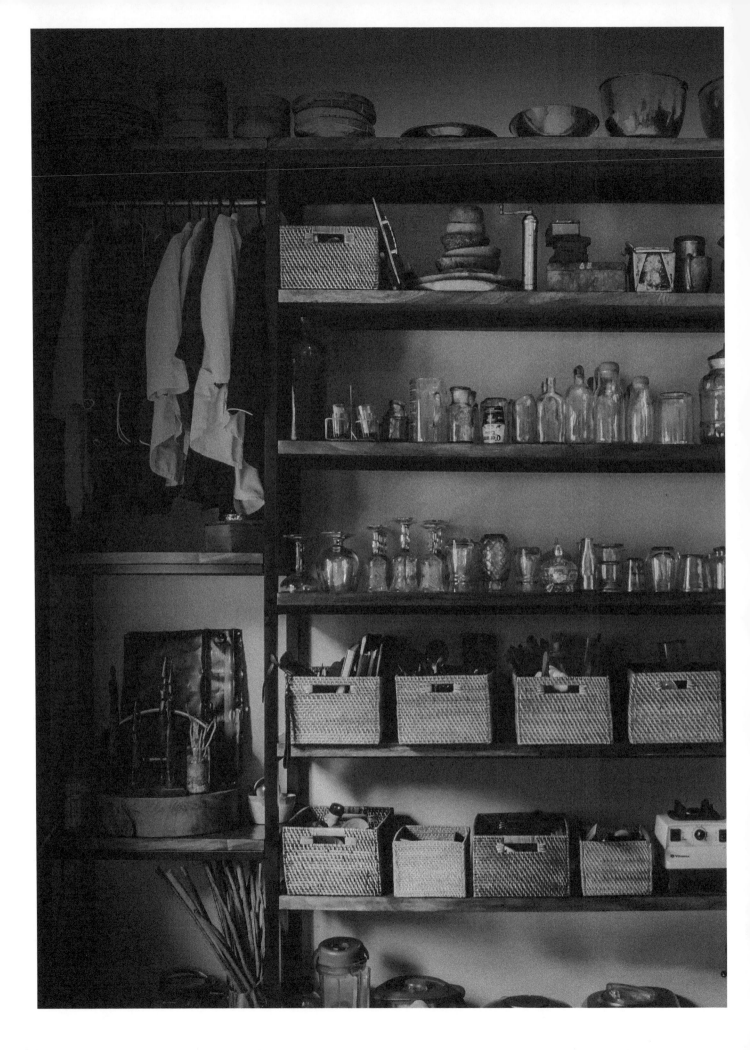

They're made to be as close to nature as possible.

Just because your super-food low-GI protein bar has superfoods and a low Glycemic Index does not mean it's digestible or absorbable. Nor will it make you feel good while you scoff it in the car rushing to work after a fight with your sweetheart.

That's superfood-ism for you. It's a set of constructed thoughts which someone else has created and you have bought into.

Don't get me wrong – superfoods are super. It's not superfood-ism that's the problem. The state of mind that tells you "I need to eat chia seeds and kale because they're healthy and slimming and I need to lose weight or no one will love me". That's the toxic process right there.

There's an intelligence in nature that we absorb when we eat food that is not processed. Food that is free from shitty salts and processed sugar and refined oils, that was grown in good soil using caring farming techniques.

Your body feels it. You recognize it, because your body comes from the same natural intelligence.

And when we stand in that intelligence, when we connect with our body, the weight naturally falls away. The skin clears up. The energy returns.

P.S. More nature. Less -isms.

Inner Health Contract

One of the greatest things I was ever told is something called your Inner Health Contract.

It's like your car insurance, but instead of paying money to know your car will be fixed, you pay with good food and good feelings and good thoughts.

Because what sort of old person do you want to be?

My dear friend Rachelle actually wrote hers out and in her case (cos everyone's different) she had a number of clauses which started with "I must…"

I must drink water
I must breathe deeply
I must satiate myself with foods I love
I must acknowledge how I feel when I eat food
I must understand how I feel

Your inner health contract might be completely different.

You've got to go by feeling. And when women and men become grounded in their body, in their presence, in the natural intelligence which runs through all things, you can ignore all the voices

and the industries around us which tell us
• don't eat this
• eat this instead
• count this
• less of that

You have the opportunity to connect with your body and make your own, unique Inner Health Contract.

I hate kale

I hate kale. I think that should be the title of a book.

I especially hate kale in green smoothies. Ergh. Pour me a glass of pureed lawn clippings in milk #vomit.

So I don't drink kale. I don't even drink smoothies because I F-ing hate smoothies! And that's part of My Inner Health Contract.

I'm not going to eat kale, and I'm definitely not going to drink it in a smoothie just because it's the latest food-ism. The latest health trend. The latest pouty yoga Insta-whatever telling me that she loves kale (#love and #blessings and #kale to all the pouty yoga IG stars out there btw – half of you are already my friends lol). I've got to let my body decide.

I've got to get really honest with how my body feels after I eat a meal.

And I've got to stick as close to nature as possible.

From that place – that place of honesty and nature – you'll discover your own Inner Health Contract.

You are F-ing amazing and never ever forget that

You are. You are f-ing amazing. Never forget that. And if you do then I'm here to remind you. Because I need to remind myself every day.

I remind myself I'm amazing through the thoughts I think, the emotions I create, the food I cook and eat.

Every day is a reminder.

I figure I've got another 50 years on this planet. I'm going to make them good ones. There will be ups and there will be downs – that's life, but we're better together, and if I can change just one more life through my cooking and my philosophy and my goddam amazing Cheesecake In A Glass or Creamy Mushroom Pasta then you know what? It will be a good life.

Thanks for joining me.

Chef Cynthia Louise xx

Don't leave your soup when it's cooking.
Give it some love, pay attention,
taste it... what does it need...

Introducing Christina Zipperlen

How a Jewellery Designer Ended up in a Cookbook

Once upon a time, an introverted artist and yogi was living in the jungles of Bali battling a rather challenging stretch of life. Somewhere in the midst of her tears she declared:

I shall not go through this alone!

Called by the woman's declaration, a shiny, cape-wrapped creature appeared. This creature was Kat Dawes (whom we shall meet later) and she offered the yogi these words of reassurance:

Fear not, my friend, for I am with you now.

Kat wasn't joking, either – she moved right on into the woman's home. Nor had she travelled alone. Oh no, she had a chef by her side. A badass, outspoken, glorious chef who spoke her mind, took over the kitchen and cooked up a storm. Those two women nourished the artist with love, friendship, support and laughter. While Kat fed her food for the mind, Cynthia fed her food for the body. If you could only see the food she fed her!

Lucky for you, since you are holding this book, you will get to see them!

Fast forward eight years and those two women are now my dearest friends, and the introverted artist – me – made it through her dark night of the soul. While Cynthia is the badass chef, all three of us have a mission to nourish this world in our own special ways, which is why she has given us the spotlight for a page or two in her glorious creation.

So, what do I mean by *nourish?*

The obvious answer, and the reason you are holding this cookbook, is the act of feeding these amazing bodies of ours with food – physical, digestible, chewable, and able-to-be-swallowed ingredients.

But in my experience, edibles are not the only form of nourishment needed. My relationship with food hasn't been the easiest.

To be honest, it has been difficult. For years I denied myself the nourishment food could give me. Instead, I starved myself. I controlled and manipulated my body by denying it the nutrition it craved to function the way it should.

I was one of many young women dealing with an eating disorder.

Through my journey to overcome anorexia I discovered the many ways humans receive and require nourishment. Nourishment is life force, which is expressed in many different forms. It can be experienced through art and writing; through breath and sunshine; through community, family, friendships, and belonging; through therapy, love, and spirituality; and through prayer, meditation, dance, and movement. Everything I've mentioned and so many more are alternate forms of nourishment for the soul and the body. And, of course, nourishment for the body comes in the form of cooking and eating. These are necessities.

Cooking and eating are two of the marvellous ways we can feed ourselves and celebrate this one precious life we get to live. To honour the amazing bodies we inhabit.

Cynthia is a wonderful and moving teacher and healer. She made a profound difference

in my life when it came to my relationship with food. Her love for cooking is contagious. In the process of learning her recipes, I learned to love my own body again.

Being around Cynthia and seeing the way she treats food brought a new understanding into my life. I learnt to celebrate the plants, the flavours, the origins of the ingredients and the farmers who grew the plants. I learnt to celebrate my body and my organs as they are nourished by the energy of real food.

Unfortunately, many of us deal with unhealthy relationships with food as well as a disproportionate amount of loneliness and isolation. Food is healing in so many ways. It is a celebration of our bodies and a tool to bring us together and create community – especially when it is made at home from pure ingredients. Cynthia not only taught me to cook, she showed me that eating nutritious food with loved ones is like an internal hug.

In return, I adorned her body with my form of nourishment.

My expression of nourishment is my art. While Cynthia nourishes bodies through her recipes, I nourish souls through jewellery. Just like Cynthia's food is *more* than food, my jewellery is more than jewellery. I work with a wonderful team of women who bless each of our creations with love and prayers. Each piece is sustainably made and gives back to the local community. Every item carries messages and meanings, reminding us to love ourselves and the ones around us. The jewellery pieces are wearable expressions of self-love and nourishment for the soul.

If you have ever met Cynthia you will notice she is covered in my creations. She has told me many times that her body can literally feel the words *You Are Loved* when she puts on each piece. This is the reason I do what I do. Just like my organs hear the loving prayers of the nourishment she packs into her recipes, I love that her body feels the same from my creations.

I am deeply grateful to know Cynthia and have the honour of being a recipient of her form of nourishment. I also celebrate that you found her work. This world needs people to discover their own form of nourishment and find creative ways to express them.

What will it take? More art? More community? More joy and celebration? More living in the Now? More spirituality? More yummy food? *(Clearly!)* Whatever it is, find it and do it. Enjoy it and live it.

> *May you always find what you need to be nourished*
> *in every way your body, heart, and soul craves.*

Christina Zipperlen, Creator & CEO of Ananda Soul

Introducing Kat Dawes
- Founder of NOWism.

When I first met Cynthia she didn't like me. We were like chalk and cheese, balancing out the universe in some bizarre way. I was painfully friendly and she was blunt and basically rude. I was enthusiastically engaged and present, Cynthia was aloof and dismissive. Though we were radically different, secretly I knew she was 'my people':

Hello dormant superhero, it is just a matter of time before we join forces to conquer the world!

When she realised it was I who had painted a big psychedelic mural of a meditating man in the car park of her restaurant she took a little more interest in me. Straight up she asked me if I would paint the ceiling of her restaurant?

"What? Like Michaelangelo did for the Sistine Chapel?"

"Yes."

"Holy now cow! #yes!" My mind exploded into a romance of possibilities.

FYI: Her business partner at the time stopped me from ever touching that ceiling but nevertheless it was the beginning of my very unique connection with Chef Cynthia Louise.

Life kept putting us in the same places at the same time. We shared plenty of mutual connections and I started to hear more about *Chef Cynthia Louise.* A chef hey? Such an alien interest to me, I lived off packets of raw nuts and dates and would hesitate deeply around boiling an egg. When I tasted her food I was blown away and I realised her spirituality lay in her relationship to food. I took an instant interest in her wisdom of plant based nourishment.

One day she abruptly made something very clear to me: "I don't want to know anything about that NOWism stuff you do. I'm not interested so don't tell me about it."

(Awkward pause.)

Alrighty then. Ten points for clear communication skills and negative ten thousand points for delivery. It sounded like she was describing something seriously filthy! By the way, NOWism is nothing other than my entire life's work! Lucky for me, in that very moment I was deep in my NOWism practice. I had some serious internal superhero skills and now I was about to unleash a demonstration. I knew I had the power to remain unbothered by this human's brutal disinterest in my soul...

Here is what happened:

As the negative #energy came at me through the invisible Mental Atmosphere I performed an internal NOWism move known as 'The Quack: Water Off A Duck's Back'. The energy (#) just slipped on past my moment and I remained #untriggered #poised #calm and #easy. The universe applauded my momentary victory and I smiled...

Ironically, I couldn't think of anyone who needed this "NOWism stuff" more than Cynthia.

Fast forward through this epic tale to the Present Moment where, just as I suspected, it turns out that Cynthia is indeed a superhero! Today this 'NOWism stuff' is found scattered throughout her life. In fact you won't be able to NOT find it! There is a trace of it literally everywhere. It's in the language she uses; the ink on her skin; behind the business deals she makes; her reverence towards her own beating heart, and of course it is in every single one of her delicious recipes.

It's the one cup of *#joy,* the one pinch of *#gratitude,* the one spoon of *#letgo* that confuses and enlightens you when you are making her recipes.

I often wonder about the questions that must come in from her fans:

"Chef Cynthia, is '#letgo a special brand of something? Where do I get it from?"

"Talk to Kat Dawes."

And now here I am in her fabulous book.

NOWism is the art of conscious participation in the present moment. It is a personal culture of mindfulness that you design into your life. Not only do you save the present moment from habitual negativity and mindless thought pollution, you also train your attention to look – relentlessly – for possibilities. As you tune into them, suddenly you see them everywhere.

You take everyday moments and make them extraordinary! #power. You tweak your perception and make corrections! #forgiveness. You disengage from stories that keep you small. #confidence. Basically, NOWism is a practice for budding superheroes. It disrupts your dormant powers into full expression!

But wait why did Cynthia, the anti-nowist, suddenly become such an active student in a mindfulness practice? What was the turning point?

It's no secret that most of us grow because of immense pain. Something happens in life and it forces us to change. "Pain pushes until the vision pulls" to quote the amazing Michael Bernard Beckwith.

Cynthia was pushed by pain. Basically, it was time for her to activate the dormant superhero powers I've been talking about. It happened during a chapter in her personal story where she had won a victory over a very serious health battle – at least that is how it first appeared. Her discipline with water fasting, sun practices, movement and breath was brilliantly successful. A group of us watched her heal in a most extraordinary way! Yet down the track, in the midst of her impeccable healthy lifestyle and alkaline food intake, that horrifying diagnosis reappeared and once again captured her full attention. As pain pushed her deep into #fear, Cynthia started asking different questions:

What am I missing?
What do I need to change?

I remember sitting with her as she unpacked this internal conflict. She had been through SO much in one lifetime she reminded me of some sort of ancient warrior.

Born with a genetic heart defect, adopted, raised in Papua New Guinea, two open heart surgeries, cancer, divorce – this woman had lived *a lot of life*. She had a hard protective exterior with a secret softness on the inside. I said to her:

"You know how you are what you eat? Well, what if you are what you THINK?"

She looked at me horrified. I had a feeling the problem wasn't *what* she was doing, it was the *way* she was doing it. The missing piece = Consciousness. Presence. Praxis. NOWism.

I have always been intrigued by the magical, invisible layers of our being. I imagine our Mental Atmosphere is alive with dynamic activity! Energy, emotion, thoughts and mind; all dancing and collaborating to make that which is in the mind – matter! Our thoughts play a much bigger role in our physical health than most people realise. Right now, even in this very moment, we are co-creating reality through the flavour of our focus. (#)

Cynthia realised on the surface she was doing all the right things to be healthy, but in the ideasphere of her mind and in the deep spaces of her heart, she was full of #fear #doubt #anger and even a dash of #rage. It's a precious moment – this one I am describing. The Game Changer. A private moment of revelation. Cynthia had a new battle to face, the invisible enemy – her internal *Momenterrorists*.

Momenterrorism is the contamination of the present moment via a **habitual** focus on #fear #doubt #lack #loss #worry #frustration etc. It becomes a subconscious event; a part of the personality. Sometimes it is known as *negative thinking*.

Facing an army of momenterrorists, the battle was real, and NOW NINJA Cynthia was ON. She dragged her attention from #fear and threw it in the general direction of #trust. She started to unhook herself from dense frequencies that were blocking her light, she cancelled her lifetime subscription to #drama and #bullshit and invested her precious attention deep into the possibilities of the present moment. Continuing the things that supported her health, she drank the water, she stood in the light, she breathed deeply but now... she also #smiled. Devoted to the quality of her participation in the present moment, she learned to build #ease #flow #gratitude #confidence #trust and started to #love herself again. She started where she was, with what she had, and she didn't stop... In perfect NOWism style, she chipped away by doing a little bit – a lot. I watched my superhero sister gradually shake herself awake.

Cynthia is a story of radical human evolution. She is the battle – fought and won! Her devotion to activating her true potential has been exhilarating to witness and I am deeply honored by the testimonial she shares about this work. I have helped hundreds of people take this *inner quest* and I have never seen someone grow and change SO much – so fast as Cynthia Louise. I am proud beyond words of the way Cynthia inspires people to turn up in their kitchens and connect with their lives and then their knives, to be unapologetic in their sense of #passion and #purpose, get over the bullshit of self-loathing and start practicing true #selflove. She's a no bullshit type of sister and her star is currently rising...

And just when you thought this story couldn't get any more rad, there is one other victory that needs to be mentioned. I now take to the kitchen like a boss. I can take nuts and dates and do extraordinary things. I make the *Neat Loaf* and the *Vegan Lasagna* and if I'm halfway through and I have burning questions I call the Chef directly. That's just one of the many perks of having your best mate be a world class chef.

Our exchange is equal. Our celebration is mutual. The story keeps getting better and I am eternally #grateful. ∞

Kat Dawes, NOWism.

Flashtags

*"Hey Cynthia, I have a question for you, in the Vegan Neat Loaf,
what is one bunch of #grateful? Is it a brand? Where can I buy that?"
Ask Kat Dawes... NOWISM #FlashTags*

#JOY

#joy is like the energy of the sun; bright, luminous it erupts from inside into a smile. "I love my life!"

#EASE&FLOW

Like water flowing in a stream, no hindrances, or delays, just an elegant stream of energy and momentum. "I am always in the right place at the right time."

#LETTINGGO

Trusting that which is no longer needed gently falls away to make room for something greater. Letting go is the art of the great surrender! "I love letting go!"

#COMFORT

A sense of softness and security. "I am exactly where I should be, in this moment NOW!"

#GRATITUDE

A sense of fullness, a realisation that I am truly blessed! Gratitude is a state of receivership! "I am so grateful for this life!"

#FORGIVENESS

A courageous decision to be alkaline in my thinking and feeling. Forgiveness creates #freedom.

#FAITH

"I may not know all things... but I know the 'knower'. I can safely take the leap because the universe has my back."

#LOVE

"Love is what I am made of, it is the cosmic glue holding the universe together. Love is my natural state. It is my most powerful me."

#COURAGE

Courage is the lion in you that moves forwards regardless of the fear. "I know the conditions will never be right, but I know I can become the right (internal) condition."

#PEACE

Behind all the busyness there is a clear field – it is always present and peaceful. "All my needs are met!"

#RESPECT

The ultimate form of self love. Whether I am respecting another or respecting myself, being connected to #respect keeps me in integrity with my soul. "I appreciate and respect life in all its variety."

#POSITIVITY

Positivity is celebration of the perfection of life! "My positive focus is an alkaline focus – it supports me in endless ways."

#ACCEPTANCE

Acceptance is the art of falling in love with where you are. "I start where I am with what I have, all things are possible from here!"

#PATIENCE

Patience is a distant cousin of #trust. It is the art of letting things unfold in their own timing. "I trust in the divine timing of my life! I am at ease while I wait."

#TRUST

It's a big vibe! One of the most valuable and precious. "Trust is knowing that I find out what I need to know – when I need to know it!"

#ABUNDANCE

It's good for me to remember, I am made from the very abundance I seek. As I train my eyes to see the availability around me – I never go without! "Grateful for the overflow of abundance in my life!"

#INSPIRATION

When I am inspired, I am in spirit! It is the high flying vibe that comes through me when I am fully present. "I am filled with inspiration, and I take action when I am inspired!"

#CONTENTMENT

Soft. Safe. Yummy. Sweet. Contentment is knowing that you are exactly where you should be in this moment in time. "Happy right where I am, and also eager for more."

#SELFWORTH

The most important romance of all time! Self worth is a life's work, we can only truly receive our heart's desire if we know we are worthy. "I was born worthy! My worth is not based on my achievements, it is based on my existence!"

#CARE

Care is presence. Undivided and intention. "As I express care, I am in a high quality, conscious participation with this moment."

Shop

When I create a recipe I start with ingredients that are as close to nature as possible. The less human interference the better.

Keep that in mind and you can't go wrong.

I also have a keen eye on creating positive change with my wallet, so I consider carefully where I spend my money – will it be the local supermarket? A farmer's market? A co-op? Or something else?

I invest deeply in the flow of energy in the process. Food makes its way from soil health to seed, planting, growing, harvesting, storing and transporting, all the way to the human being I hand over my hard-earned cash to.

I am well aware of the power my wallet has on the planet. Every purchase I make creates a ripple effect, so I want to do so with the best of intentions, being mindful of the entire process all the way back to the health of the soil where it all starts.

I enjoy shaking the hand that will feed me and my friends, my family and my clients. I might do this physically, and I always do it energetically with my wallet. Every dollar is like a vote for natural, whole ingredients that are grown organically or biodynamically.

As a passionate advocate for ethical farming practices and soil regeneration I will actively seek out farmers and products that are part of this process.

I translate their wisdom and love of growing our food into my recipes with a genuine respect and care for the journey.

Farmers are one of the main solutions to the health of my organs, my whole body, my students, friends and my community. Regenerative farming and practices which preserve and regenerate the health of the soil ensure that this vitality will be preserved for generations to come, and in turn provides us with incredible "living supplements" – edible plants for our dinner table which nourish us.

These are some of the things which pass through my mind as I shop. My internal teacher (my in-tuition) guides my eyes across everything on the shop floor and tells me immediately what has been processed, what has lost its vitality somewhere in the chain, and what remains vibrant and connected to life. I have spent 25 years of my life cultivating this practice to teach people to choose produce which feed you, nourish you, and support everyone around you all the way back to the soil in which it springs from.

Real food as close to nature as nature intended with low human interference.

In the Pantry

I only have one criteria for my ingredients which makes it really easy.

All my ingredients are biodynamic or organic.

Organic food is farmed without synthetic chemicals, growth promoters, hormones or genetically modified components. It's better for the soil, better for the planet and better for you.

Biodynamic food is even better. It's organic food which is holistically cultivated according to a set of natural principles to replenish the soil and create a sustainable enterprise.

If it so happens that I can't find biodynamic or organic food then I don't panic either. I'd rather stress less, make do with what's available and look a bit harder next time.

HERE'S WHAT YOU'LL FIND IN MY PANTRY.

SPICES

Allspice

Allspice is the dried brown berry of the tropical Pimenta Dioica tree which is a relative of the clove.

Cayenne pepper

Always go for biodynamic or organic cayenne pepper because they are stronger in flavour.

Chili flakes

I make my own chili flakes by drying them in a dehydrator and blending them quickly in my Vitamix to keep a bit of flakey texture.

Chili powder (Kashmiri)

This can be swapped out for common chilli powder so don't stress if you can't find it

Cinnamon powder

Super easy to make your own cinnamon powder. Break up cinnamon bark into chunks, blend them in a high-speed blender and pass them through a sieve.

Cumin powder

I make my own cumin powder by toasting cumin seeds in a pan and grinding them in my blender. The flavour is stronger this way. If you can't

be bothered you can buy biodynamic or organic cumin powder.

Coriander powder

I make my own coriander powder using the method I use for making cumin powder. Same rules apply.

Curry powder

I use a mild, balanced curry powder that is on the sweeter side and not the spicy side

Oregano

Use dried leaves, not a powder

Paprika (smoked and sweet)

A staple in my pantry because I love the smokey flavour it gives to meals. I also use sweet paprika too.

Pepper

The best pepper to use in cooking is freshly cracked. I buy a large amount of good quality peppercorns and grind them myself so I always have it on tap when I need it.

Porcini powder

I make my own by buying mushrooms which have been sliced and dried. I add them to the vitamix, press play and there I have the powder

Salt

Don't stick to one type. Change it up as much as you can. The reason is simple – different types of salt have different combinations of minerals, and you shouldn't deny your body any of these. My go-to salt is pink Himalayan salt, but I also use Bali sea salt, or black salt.

Turmeric powder

I love turmeric because it's so versatile and you can use it not only in savoury dishes but also in drinks. It's known for its anti-inflammatory properties, the earthy flavour it gives to meals and its vibrant colour.

Vanilla seeds

These are simply the seeds that are dried and bottled

Vanilla pods

Long fresh semi-dried pods. I use the seeds together with the pod by cutting it into 2cm slices and either chucking them into the blender of popping them in to a drink as is

Vanilla extract

Find a brand that is not filled with sugar.

SWEETENERS

Coconut sugar

I have very good coconut sugar

made in Indonesia. Make sure that you choose a pure one with as little human interference as possible.

Dates

Dried dates are the best natural sweetener for your desserts and drinks.

Maple syrup

I use pure maple syrup and I love it. It's gorgeous!

Sultanas

Always choose ones without sulphur and oil.

VINEGAR AND MUSTARD

Apple cider vinegar.

My brand of choice is Braggs. They have amazing organic apple cider vinegar which contains the mother

Balsamic vinegar

I use the brands from Modena, Italy

Mustard (Dijon and Yellow mustard)

Read the jar carefully and look for real ingredients (mustard, apple cider vinegar, salt etc.). Avoid anything with flavours, additives or sugar.

Umeboshi plum vinegar

My number one choice is umeboshi vinegar from Spiral Foods.

CACAO PRODUCTS

I always choose organic products from Fairtrade.

Cacao powder

Cacao paste

Cacao nibs

SEEDS, NUTS, LENTILS, GRAINS, BUTTERS AND FLOURS

Almond meal

I sometimes make my own almond meal by grinding almonds.

Besan or chickpea flour

Brown lentils

Buckwheat flour

When I have buckwheat kernels I grind them and make my own buckwheat flour.

Cassava flour

Gluten-free breadcrumbs

Gluten-free flour

My favourite brand is Bob's Red Mill.

Pressed oats

Psyllium husk

Raw amaranth seeds

Raw and unhulled tahini

Raw black sesame seeds

Raw cashews

Raw chia seeds

Raw fenugreek seeds

Raw flax seeds

Raw hemp seeds

Raw mustard seeds

Raw pecans

Raw pumpkin seeds

Raw quinoa

Raw sunflower seeds

Raw walnuts

Raw white sesame seeds

Red split peas

Rice flour

Roasted almond butter

Roasted peanut butter

White long-grain rice

OIL

Toasted sesame oil

The brand I recommend is Spiral Foods.

Cold-pressed olive oil

Cold-pressed, non-deodorised, unfiltered coconut oil

MILK

Any plant-based milk e.g. oat milk, almond milk, soy milk.

Look for milk that's as pure as possible. I encourage you to make milk on your own but if you choose to buy, check the label and opt for one with ingredients as close to nature as possible.

COCONUT PRODUCTS

Coconut cream

The brand I truly trust is Kara.

Cultured coconut yogurt

Buy the purest one you can find.

Desiccated coconut

The best one is without any sulphur. Bob's Red Mill is the brand I recommend.

Coconut flakes

As with desiccated coconut, the best product out there is the one without sulphur. I like Bob's Red Mill products.

BITS AND PIECES

Activated charcoal

Baking powder

My preferred brand is Bob's Red Mill.

Dried rosella flower

Goji berries

Choose ones without sulphur and oil.

Liquid smoke

Red wine

I always use biodynamic, preservative-free wine.

Rice paper

Savoury yeast

Soy sauce/tamari

I use the salt-reduced one from Spiral Foods.

Tomato paste

Tomato puree

Unpasteurised shiro miso paste

Spiral Foods is my choice.

Equipment

Here's a little secret about my equipment – there is no secret!

I get by with basically a food processor, a blender, and a whole pile of cast iron and stainless steel pots and pans. Some of them I got from a chef store, sometimes I snagged them at the local op shop.

You should know by now that I prefer natural. That means no non-stick surfaces for me. Stainless steel and wood where possible. Glass mason jars for storing things in. And a gas stove. Because it's the closest thing we'll get to having a campfire at home.

My one fancy piece is that I have a display fridge with glass doors. Apart from that there ain't nothing I have that you can't get.

HERE'S WHAT I USE DAILY:

MACHINES & THINGS

Blender – Vitamix 5200

Food Processor – Magimix 5200

Cast iron pans

Stainless steel pots

Utensils – stainless steel or wood

Storage containers – glass clip jars or mason jars

Gas stove top

Gas oven

There you have it. No fancy whatchamacallits, doodads or extra isms. Nothing that slices, dices, peels and plucks. No AI-controlled thermamixes. Apart from a slight obsession with a good knife which is a must – it's just fire, natural materials, a bit of help from the blender and a whole lotta good vibes and love.

KNIVES

I'm a stickler for a nice knife. Like your mind, you want it to be sharp! That means you also need to be #mindful when you're using them.

Mindfulness lies at the heart of everything, just like a good knife is at the heart of every kitchen. Here's what I use:

Knife 1 – 10 inch blade
Brand = Shun
Hand crafted and made in Japan from Damascus steel

Knife 2 – 8 inch blade
Brand = Miyabi
Made in Japan from High Carbon CMB60 steel

Knife 3 – 4 inch blade
Brand = Victorinox
Diamond Head Steel for sharpening

CHOPPING BOARD

Made from recycled wood, 60cm long and 40cm wide. I get this sanded twice a year.

Nourish your 3 brains.
Head brain, heart brain, gut brain.

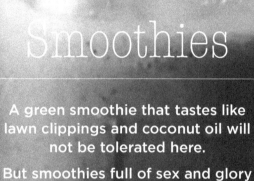

Smoothies

A green smoothie that tastes like
lawn clippings and coconut oil will
not be tolerated here.

But smoothies full of sex and glory
or with names like Cheesecake In A Glass
– now I'm all about that!

Get a taste of these situations
– they will change your life.

Sexy Nutty

*I went to a cafe in Uluwatu on the southern tip of Bali and ordered
an oat cacao peanut butter situation. I was like:*

Okay, this is good, now go home and recreate this glory to a better glory.

So I did it.

*Epic is the word that describes this smoothie.
I wanted it to be thick and rich in flavour, so I ended up adding more cacao.
It was so good that I basically felt like diving into the glass immediately.*

Ingredients

2 tbsp cacao powder
3 tbsp peanut butter
1 frozen banana
1/4 cup oats
1 cup coconut milk
Sweetener of your choice,
as much as you like
1 tray of ice
A pinch of salt
1 cup #GRATITUDE

Method

Add The ingredients to your blender and blend until smooth.

Enjoy!

PREP TIME 2-3 mins
FREEZER-FRIENDLY No
R, RSF

MAKES 2

Cheesecake in a Glass

It was way back when I created this beauty for the first time. A couple of friends popped down for a visit to give me a hand in my studio. I served this lassi and my friend Nicci took one sip, looked back at me and asked:

WTF is this?

I shared my secret recipe and she continued to slurp away with so much love in her eyes.

In her words, this lassi is like a cheesecake in a cup and it is frigging epic. The word on the street is that she hasn't stopped talking about and craving it. Well, now it's here for you, Nicci and the rest of the world to enjoy!

Ingredients

1/3 cup coconut yogurt
1 cup ice
1/4 cup freshly squeezed lemon juice
1/4 cup maple syrup
2 tsp freshly grated ginger
1 tsp freshly grated turmeric
A pinch of #COURAGE

Method

Add all the ingredients to your blender and blend until well combined.

Serve and enjoy!

PREP TIME 2-3 mins
FREEZER-FRIENDLY No
R, RSF, NF

SERVES 1

Choco Maca

This one is for you, Courtney. We've always shared so much passion over this creation. The moment it hits your lips, it sends your taste buds flowing and you just can't help but move that body and celebrate how utterly delicious it is! I can't even count how much joy this drink has brought to us over many years.

I hope that when you make this recipe, it makes your heart sing and your body dance like it does for Courtney and myself.

Ingredients

2 tbsp cacao powder
1/4 cup cashew nuts
2 tsp maca powder
1 cup water
Maple syrup or coconut sugar, as much as you like
2 trays of ice
A pinch of salt
1 tbsp #JOY

Method

Add all the ingredients to your blender and blend until well combined.

Serve and enjoy!

PREP TIME 2-3 mins
FREEZER-FRIENDLY No
R, RSF

SERVES 2

OMG Goji

Refreshing and orange in colour, this drink screams of gojiiiii!
If you're not a fan of goji, use dried strawberries instead. #beyondyum

Ingredients

1/4 cup almonds, soaked for
6 hours or overnight and
rinsed well.
1/3 cup goji berries
1/2 tsp vanilla powder
4 dates, pitted
3 oranges, juiced
2 trays of ice
A pinch of salt
1 cup #PATIENCE

Method

Add all the ingredients to your blender and blend until smooth and creamy.

Take a deep breath and enjoy your drink!

PREP TIME 2-3 mins
FREEZER-FRIENDLY No
R, RSF

MAKES 750 ML

Give me the chocolate
and no-one gets hurt.

Blackberry Parsley

This drink is weird and awesome. Berries and bananas are a common smoothie combination and you can't go wrong here. I froze them first because I found that this adds a bit more creaminess to smoothies. Plus, I don't need to use extra ice.

Anyways, how did parsley find its way into this smoothie? Easily! Herbs are packed with heaps of epic isms but we often forget about them. So adding them to smoothies is a sneaky way to enrich your diet.

You may think that adding parsley will ruin your perfect, purple drink but trust me on this one. Give it a try and you'll find that the flavour of parsley is not overpowering at all.

Cheers!

Ingredients

1 cup firmly packed
flat-leaf parsley
1 cup frozen blackberries
1 frozen banana
1 cup water
Maple syrup, as much
as you wish
A pinch of salt
1 cup #CONTENTMENT

Method

Add the ingredients to your blender and blend until smooth and creamy.

Treat yourself!

PREP TIME 2-3 mins
FREEZER-FRIENDLY No
R, RSF, NF

SERVES 1

Banana Milkshake of Glory

What makes this milkshake better than yours? LOL It's the dried bananas, baby.
This is the trick to having a rich, banana flavour that has an incredible depth.
It's a crowd-pleaser and both the small and the big kids in your life will love it.

Ingredients

1/2 tsp vanilla powder
1 frozen banana
A handful of dried bananas
1 cup coconut milk, or any
other nut milk of choice
2 big handfuls of ice
A pinch of salt
1 tbsp #SELFWORTH

Method

Add all the ingredients to your blender and blend until smooth and well combined.

Serve and enjoy!

PREP TIME 2-3 mins
FREEZER-FRIENDLY No
R, RSF, NF

SERVES 1

We eat. We don't .
And we nourish ourselves.

Breakfast

I have so much gratitude for real food. Food that our farmers spend countless hours growing for us. Food that has its place in the human body. And meals formed by joyful moments and memories that can last a lifetime.

How we think, eat, and feel about ourselves matters. What you eat matters. We are all so worth taking care of.

This is how breakfast is served.

Eggless Omelette

Shut the front door. Close the gate. Lock up the house. Return to your kitchens vegan people. I friggin' love this dish! Those crispy edges and the middle that's as light as a feather brings a smile to my mates face. Be mindful though that changing the flour will change the entire dish. So let's all stick to the plan, right?

When making this omelette keep in mind that you are after a batter that resembles pancake batter. Otherwise your omelette will fall apart if you add too much liquid.

I'd love to see the surprise on your face when you take a bite of this eggless omelette and realise that it tastes like eggs. It's actually the black salt, which is rich in sulphur, that gives the egg taste to your eggless breakfast. It's amazing!

This one's for all my vegan mates who are vegan! Shower with fresh cherry tomatoes, tear up some greens with fresh herbs, add my balsamic glaze and you have an absolute joy of a dish to master and EAT.

Ingredients

300g soft or silken tofu
1 shallot, peeled
1 garlic clove, peeled
1 tbsp savoury yeast
1/3 cup plant milk
1/2 cup rice flour
1/2 tsp turmeric powder
A pinch of black salt
Salt and black pepper,
to taste
Coconut oil, for frying
1 tbsp #FAITH

FOR SERVING:

Fresh mixed lettuce and
fresh herbs
Cherry tomatoes, halved
Balsamic glaze

Method

Add the ingredients to a blender, blend till it resembles the same texture as a pancake batter and set aside.

Heat some oil on medium-high, pour in half of the omelette mixture and cook until the surface starts bubbling up, the omelette is cooked through and the edges are crispy. There is no need to flip the omelette.

Repeat the same with the remaining batter.

Serve your eggless omelette with mixed lettuce, fresh herbs, cherry tomatoes, and a splash of balsamic glaze.

PREP TIME 5 mins
COOKING TIME 10 mins
FREEZER-FRIENDLY No
C, RSF, NF

SERVES 2

French Toast

Picture this – I was in my studio getting ready to film another recipe when one of the cameramen asked: What are we making today? I was like sh*t, not sure. We had a quick scan around the kitchen and decided to give the classic French toast a crack. Innovative: yes. Classic: no!

We looked at each other and I remember thinking: Hope this works.

And boy did it work! It was magnificent!

Here's a tip: watch the heat on this recipe as the almond meal tends to burn. Cook it slowly and adjust the heat up and down to get it a bit crispy around the edges. The toppings that I use are essential as they make everything come together in a truly tasty, epic way.

Report back on my social media with your pics and thoughts on this sweet, yummy goodness.

Ingredients

FOR THE TOAST

1 cup coconut milk or any other plant-based milk
1/2 tsp vanilla extract
1/4 tsp cinnamon powder
1/2 tsp allspice
2 tbsp almond meal
4 slices sourdough or gluten-free bread
A pinch of salt
Coconut oil, for frying

FOR THE TOPPINGS:

1/4 cup pecans
1 punnet raspberry, sliced
3 strawberries, cut into quarters
2 tbsp cacao nibs
4 tbsp coconut yogurt
Maple syrup, as much as you like
A pinch of #INSPIRATION

PREP TIME 5 mins
COOKING TIME 10-15 mins
FREEZER-FRIENDLY No
C, RSF

Method

Heat a pan on medium-low.

Whisk together the milk, vanilla and spices and let it steep for 5 minutes.

Strain, discard spice bits and stir in the almond meal.

Add the bread slices (one at a time) to the infused milk and allow them to soak the liquid.

Add a splash of coconut oil to the hot pan and fry the bread slices until golden brown and crispy around the edges on both sides.

Top with the pecans, strawberrise and raspberries.

Sprinkle with cacao nibs, drizzle with coconut yogurt and maple syrup and enjoy!

SERVES 4

One bowl, one spoon, one tin and bake.
Much love to you, your organs and your baking.

Lighten Up Loaf

Lighten Up premix loaf has all organic ingredients that are grown in rich mineral soils filled with our earth's incredible nutrients. It is the true natural mineral supplement of our time. It is the ultimate digestive healthy high fiber premix loaf that is designed to cleanse the buildup in the colon. And taste freakin EPIC.

From great soil, health is inevitable. Lighten Up Loaf is a gift from the earth to your kitchen and your belly. It's wheat and yeast free, simple and lets you Win At Baking in your own home.

It's also simple enough that anyone can mix it, stuff it in the oven and pull out an aromatic, tasty loaf which smells good, tastes great, and is digestible, nourishing, cleansing and fantastic for your insides.

Let's take a minute to acknowledge the energy behind this parcel of goodness and how it gets to your table:

Blessings to our farmers that maintain such rich nutritious soil, to the seed that grew each plant, to the pickers and to the truck drivers that delivered it.

To my manufacturer that blended the ingredients and everyone involved in the creation of real whole food goodness, Thank you!

Get yours here: chefcynthialouise.com/shop

Chef Cynthia Louise xx

FOR THE BREAD:

1 packet Lighten Up Bread Mix
(see the link below)

TOPPING IDEAS:

Almond Butter + Banana + Maple + Himalayan Salt
Seed Butter + Black Tahini
Mashed Avocado + Purple Sauerkraut
My Pro-B + Red Onion + Tomato + Olives
Mashed Avocado + Grilled Mushrooms
Hummus + Sun-dried Tomatoes + Sprouts
Smoked Tofu + Avocado + Seeds
Scrambled Tofu + Grilled Mushrooms
Hummus + Kimchi + Sprouts
My Pro-B +

chefcynthialouise.com/shop

Amaranth Porridge

Amaranth is a tall plant with big, broad, green leaves and bright flowers. There are 60 plant species belonging to the Amaranth family but we only cultivate three for seeds. Amaranth is often referred to as a grain as it has similar nutritional properties when it's raw and cooked.

I was introduced to this glorious plant in the early 90's when I was into growing my own food. What's super interesting about this exquisite plant is that it's been around for 6 to 8 thousand years. I know, right! It's a bloody long time.

The gardeners I know tell me that the Aztec, Mayan, and Inca civilisations cultivated amaranth for that long and it has been used in beautiful Mexican recipes for many years.

The flavour of amaranth is earthy and nutty. It's an exceptional replacement for oats, and believe it or not it makes for a wonderful risotto. This seed is loaded with wonderful fiber and protein but is also gluten-free. The great minds of nutritional science found out that amaranth is a complete protein. There are 9 grams of protein per one cup. Can you imagine? So much protein in this little seed.

Anyhoo... we're not giving a nutrition lecture here. Especially not when Nature's got that all sorted for us. We're here to take what Nature has provided in all her wisdom and create incredibly tasty situations to enjoy.

Amaranth is a stunning seed and when grown organically it's not only good for our health, it has a positive effect on the planet too.

Ingredients

3 slices ginger
1 cinnamon stick
1/2 tsp vanilla seeds
1/4 cup sultanas or any dried fruit of your choice
1 cup amaranth seeds
3 cups of water
Coconut milk, for serving
Toppings of your choice, for serving
A pinch of #RESPECT

Method

Add all the porridge ingredients to a pot and bring to the boil.

Simmer for 25-30 minutes with the lid on and keep stirring to prevent burning.

Serve with coconut milk, bananas, pumpkin seeds, cacao nibs and a splash of maple syrup or any other toppings you like.

PREP TIME 5 mins
COOKING TIME 8-10 mins
FREEZER-FRIENDLY No
C, RSF, NF

SERVES 2-4

Socca

This delicious savoury pancake has a lovely, slightly earthy flavour, smooth, moist interior and crispy browned edges. This was my introduction to socca: I remember seeing a message come in from my dear friend Donna (who happens to be a fabulous cook). You should make socca for your next online class. I replied with What the... and Donna was quick to send me the recipe followed with the note Make that better! I scanned through the ingredients briefly and there was one that stood out. It was besan or chickpea flour. I had to write back: Mate... I'm not a fan of besan flour unless it's filled with other isms to disguise its strong earthy flavour. Donna was relentless; she replied simply and swiftly: Make the socca and make it better!!

Our friendship is one that has an unexpected, delicious surprise. Years ago, I got a private message from a chef named Travis. He was in Bali (where I live – #soblessed) and had heard about me because his wife at that time had my cookbook (I am a co-author of 3 cookbooks with Dr Libby Weaver — another story for another time). He wanted to meet me in person to learn the art of plant-based cooking and I have to say Travis is a brilliant chef. He's extremely good, like really, really good.

Long story short, after chatting, Travis came to my villa and we cooked, ate the food and learnt a lot from each other. Months passed and Travis was heading back to New Zealand so he threw a party and invited me. It was there where he introduced me to his long-time friend Donna.

Donna and I have been friends ever since. She helped me source all the bits and pieces that now make up the kitchen studio featured in this book. When I was one cameraman down she stepped in and filmed my first series In the Raw.

Since those early days, Donna has been not only a dear friend but also a mentor and guided me throughout my career. She has a wonderful and diverse palate and is one of the best cooks I know. And her dry humour has me in stitches in the kitchen.

Beyond being a blast to hang out with, Donna has held me in the darkest times of my life and has great words of wisdom when I needed them most. She pulls me up when I'm out of line and is one of a handful of people who can understand my spelling and grammar.

This one's for you Donna!

Ingredients

FOR THE SOCCA

1 1/2 cups besan flour
1 tbsp shiro miso (white)
1 tbsp olive oil
1 1/4 cup water
Salt and black pepper,
to taste
Coconut oil, for frying
1 tbsp #GRATITUDE

FOR THE TOPPING

2 radishes, thinly sliced
A handful of fresh dill leaves
Cherry tomatoes halved
A handful of rocket
A handful of coriander
leaves

Method

TO PREPARE THE SOCCA

Whisk together all the ingredients to make a smooth pancake batter. Leave the batter to rest in the fridge overnight.

Heat a pan and add coconut oil.

Pour in 1/3 cup of the batter and cook until bubbles start appearing on the top.

Flip and cook on another side until brown and crispy around the edges.

Repeat the same with the remaining batter.

TO PREPARE THE TOPPINGS

Mix together all the ingredients.

Top the socca pancakes with the salad.

Serve with a splash of balsamic glaze.

PREP TIME 5 mins
(the batter needs overnight resting)
COOKING TIME 5 mins
FREEZER-FRIENDLY No
C, RSF, NF

SERVES 4

Tofu Scrambled

*There are so many vegan recipes for scrambled eggs and this is not one of them!
I'm not trying to replace eggs here. What I had in mind when I created this tofu scramble
is to create something packed with isms and awesomeness that my vegan friends will
wholeheartedly enjoy for breakfast. LOL.*

So here is my version of your Instagram-ready / not-scrambled eggs / tofu-vegan situation.

*To all my vegan crew: this one is for you. You know who you are so enjoy,
post your pics and tag your non-vegan friends like me!! Love xx*

Ingredients

Olive or coconut oil, for sautéing

1 packet medium tofu, crumbled

6 mushrooms, roughly chopped

1/4 red capsicum, small dice

3 spring onions, thinly sliced

2 tomatoes, small dice

1/2 cup fresh basil leaves, roughly chopped

1/2 cup fresh parsley leaves, roughly chopped

1/2 bunch of baby spinach, thinly sliced

Salt and black pepper, to taste

1 tsp #CARE

Method

Add a splash of oil in a pan and heat on high.

Add the tofu, mushrooms, capsicum, and spring onions. Season with salt and pepper, cook for 30-40 seconds and then turn down the heat to low.

Stir in the tomatoes, basil, parsley, and baby spinach and sauté while stirring continuously.

Taste, season if needed and cook for 5 more minutes or until cooked through.

Serve and enjoy!

PREP TIME 5-8 mins
COOKING TIME 10 mins
FREEZER-FRIENDLY No
C, RSF, NF

SERVES 2-3

Yellow Fritters

Food is so powerful and rich in stories. This recipe has a special story all of its own.

Way back in the day a lovely Ibu (which means mother or mum in Indonesian) taught me how to make fragrant corn fritters. Her kitchen was fascinating: there were zero benches and no electrical equipment. Just a simple fireplace on the floor, a round, wooden chopping board, a super sharp handmade knife and a mortar and a pestle made from volcanic rocks.

I found myself sitting on the kitchen floor with my legs crossed ripping husks off the corn she grew in her garden. Without uttering a word she pointed to the knife, chopping board, and corn, and I understood what my next task was. Ibu gathered up the bits of the corn I chopped, added them to her mortar together with a handful of firecracker chillies and fragrant spices and started pounding them until they turned into a rich paste.

It was the background for the most glorious corn fritters I've ever tasted in my life.

Ibu's story is rich in flavour, kindness, family, and religion and it reminds me that cooking alongside other cultures is one of the most rewarding experiences in my life. As I remember the fragrances and sounds in Ibu's kitchen I feel extremely humbled.

Now I invite you to take some aromatic ingredients, crush them in your hand, close your eyes, and smell the fragrances. Be present in the moment, be grateful for the kitchen you have and feel connected to an eternal line of earthen kitchens and wise, wise women stretching far back in to history.

Ingredients

2 corn cobs, kernels removed
A bunch of fresh coriander, roughly chopped*
3 kaffir lime leaves, finely chopped
3 spring onions, green part, finely chopped
1 red or green chili, thinly chopped
2 big garlic cloves, minced
1 tsp cumin powder
1/2 cup rice flour
2 tbsp psyllium husk
Salt and black pepper, to taste
A splash of water
Coconut oil, for frying
A pinch of #ABUNDANCE
*Use any other herbs you like

PREP TIME 5 mins
COOKING TIME 10 mins
FREEZER-FRIENDLY Yes
C, RSF, NF

Method

Add everything to your food processor, pulse to combine but keep the texture chunky.

Season with salt and pepper and mix to combine.

Heat a BBQ plate, grill or frying pan and brush it with some coconut oil.

Ladle the batter on the hot pan (use 1/3 cup as a measure) and fry until golden brown.

Flip and fry on the other side until cooked through.

Repeat with the remaining mixture. Serve and enjoy!

MAKES 6 FRITTERS

Naked Pancakes

This is for all buckwheat lovers out there, and for the non-buckwheat lovers, too (like my entire team) LOL We don't judge here... That's all I have to say about this light and fluffy ism.

Ingredients

1 cup buckwheat flour
1 tsp vanilla extract
2 1/2 tsp baking powder
1/2 banana
400ml coconut milk
1 tbsp apple cider vinegar
1-2 tbsp maple syrup
A pinch of salt
Coconut oil, for frying
Coconut yogurt, for serving
Maple syrup, for serving
1 tbsp #LOVE

Method

Add all the ingredients to your blender and blend until well combined.

Heat a pan on medium and add a splash of coconut oil.

To make a single pancake, scoop 1/3 cup of the batter, pour onto the hot pan and fry until the surface starts bubbling up.

Carefully lift up the pancake with a spatula, flip it and cook on the other side for a minute.

Repeat with the remaining batter.

Serve with a generous dollop of coconut yogurt and a splash of maple syrup.

PREP TIME 5-8 mins
COOKING TIME 4-6 mins
FREEZER-FRIENDLY No
C, RSF, NF

MAKES 8

Nourish your organs.

Chia Seed Situation

Chia seeds are such glorious tiny isms that nature has gifted us. If you are new to these seeds you'll be surprised how fast they soak up milk and transform it into a pudding situation. When I was making this for the first time I craved for some chocolate, so a couple of tablespoons of pure cacao powder found their way into this recipe.

Anyways, you can enjoy this chia pudding as it is and trust me on this next bit: take it up a notch and top it with other isms. My faves are definitely peanut butter and chocolate chips, and I feel this is what makes the recipe so inviting. Oh, and of course #LOVE.

If you're feeling adventurous I dare you to make your own peanut butter. I have to say I felt so proud after making a batch and witnessing Gun Gun (my brilliant photographer) scraping the leftovers out of the Vitamix. For those of you who don't know, the man behind the camera shooting my food creations for over 8 years is a full-blown healthy plant-eater and he knows his food well.

Back to our chia situation: don't think twice about it, just make it and nourish yourself with this glory!

Ingredients

500ml coconut milk
1/2 cup chia seeds
2-3 tbsp cacao powder
Maple syrup or coconut sugar, as much as you like
A pinch of salt
Peanut butter, for serving
Chocolate chips, for serving
1 tbsp #LETTINGGO

Method

Pour the coconut milk into a bowl.

Add the chia seeds, cacao powder, your sweetener of choice and a pinch of salt.

Whisk for at least 3-5 minutes and then transfer into a big bowl.

Top with peanut butter and chocolate chips and serve.

PREP TIME 7-10 mins
FREEZER-FRIENDLY Yes
C, RSF

SERVES 3

Smoothie bowls

You're probably wondering where the hell is the granola in these smoothie bowls?
Fun fact: smoothie bowls were invented in Brazil back in the '70s and they were made
only with frozen açai pulp and banana. Well that's what my Brazilian mates tell me.

Anyways, these smoothie bowls are a great start for your day but they are also
a perfect snack, especially if you want to trick your kids into eating more plants.
I start salivating the moment I think about a bowl filled with a thick, rich,
ice-creamy combo of goodness. I love letting my creativity go wild
and adding all sorts of isms on top that my body craves for.

A very important tip I want to give you is to use a high-speed blender when making
smoothie bowls. You can learn how to master working with blenders in my online
cooking classes. Another thing to keep in mind is that you shouldn't add any plant-based
milk or water because you want your smoothie bowl to be thick, like really #thick.

Tag me on social media so that I can admire your work.

You're welcome

Ingredients

DRAGON BOWL

2 frozen bananas, roughly chopped

1/2 frozen dragon fruit, roughly chopped

A pinch of salt

A dash of sweetener of choice, I used 1 tsp maple syrup

1 tbsp #EASE & FLOW

TROPICAL BOWL

2 frozen bananas, roughly chopped

1 cup frozen pineapple chunks

1 cup frozen mango chunks

A dash of sweetener of choice, I used 1 tsp maple syrup

A pinch of #LOVE

CHOCOLATE BOWL

2 frozen bananas, roughly chopped

2 tbsp almond butter

A pinch of salt

1 tsp vanilla extract

1-2 tbsp cacao powder

1/4 tsp turmeric powder

A dash of sweetener of choice, I used 1 tsp maple syrup

1 cup #POSITIVITY

BERRY BOWL

2 frozen bananas, roughly chopped

2 cups frozen mixed berries

A dash of sweetener of your choice, I used 1 tsp maple syrup

A pinch of salt

1 tbsp #COMFORT

Method

Whichever bowl you decide to make, remember that a high-speed blender is the gig here. I use the Vitamix. It has never failed me

Add the ingredients to your blender and blend until thick and creamy.

Transfer to a bowl and garnish with seeds, granola and toppings of your choice.

Serve and enjoy!

PREP TIME 5 mins
FREEZER-FRIENDLY Yes
R, RSF

SERVES 2

Chocolate bowl

Dragon bowl

Berry bowl

Tropical bowl

gotta go by feeling.

Balsamic Glaze

Green Ranch

Sauces &
Dressings

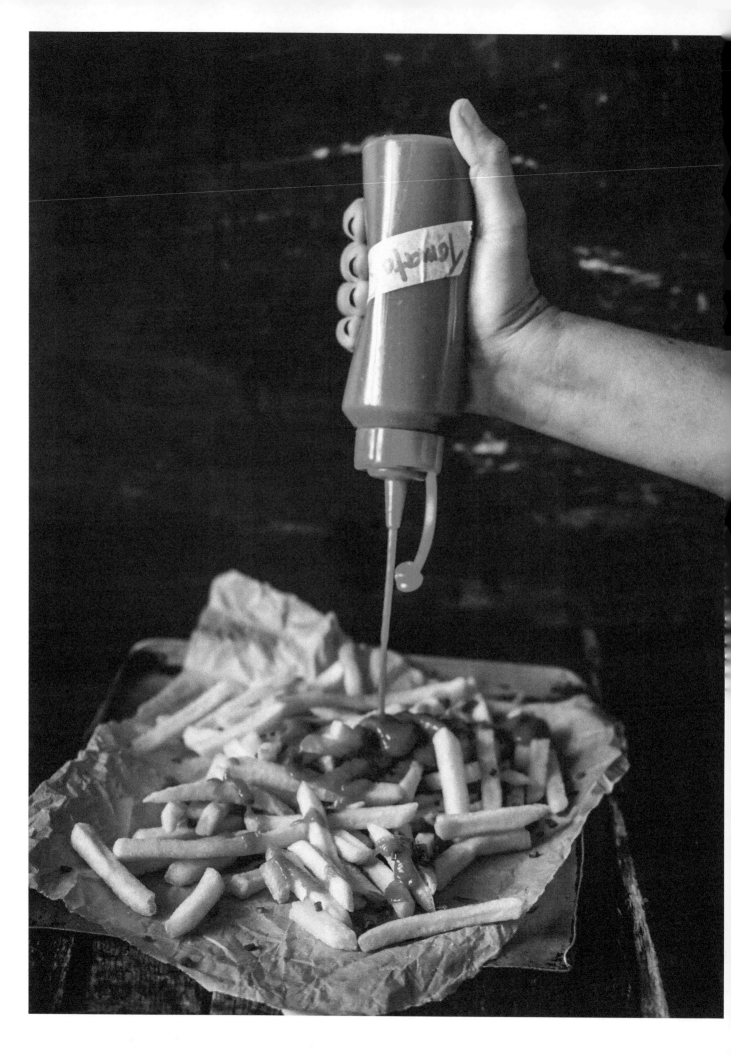

Tomato Sauce

Yes, you can buy tomato sauce in almost any store, so why bother making one of your own? With homemade tomato sauce you get an amazing opportunity to go to a farmers' market, shake the hand of the dedicated farmer who brings food to you and then buy some overripe, red and delicious tomatoes. That impact alone is, in my opinion, transformational.

Ingredients

500g red ripe tomatoes, quartered

1/2 red capsicum, roughly chopped

2 garlic cloves, smashed

1/2 onion, roughly chopped

2 tbsp apple cider vinegar

1/4 cup tomato paste, optional

2 tbsp maple syrup, or as much as you want

1/2 cup water

10ml #JOY

Method

Add the ingredients to a pot on medium.

Allow the sauce to simmer with the lid on for about 20-35 minutes or until all the liquid has evaporated.

When done, let the sauce rest for a few minutes.

Transfer to your blender and blend until smooth.

Store in a glass jar and keep in the fridge for up to 10 days

PREP TIME 2 mins
COOKING TIME 20 -35 mins
FREEZER-FRIENDLY Yes
C, RSF, NF

MAKES 300 ML

Teriyaki Sauce

This is my fav dipping sauce to serve with Donna's Balls.
It's very versatile so I use it as a dipping sauce for spring rolls,
drizzled over grilled tofu, and as a sauce for marinating eggplant.

Ingredients

20g fresh ginger, grated
2 tsp maple syrup
1/4 cup apple cider vinegar
1/4 cup tamari
1/4 cup water
1 tbsp #CARE

Method

Add the ingredients to a small pot and cook on medium for 5-8 minutes or until the mixture thickens.

Let the sauce cool and store in a glass jar in the fridge for up to 2 weeks.

PREP TIME 2 mins
COOKING TIME 5-8 mins
FREEZER-FRIENDLY Yes
R, RSF, NF

MAKES 1/2 CUP

Anti-Inflammatory Dressing

*This is the most delicious dressing I've ever made in my entire life.
Yes, I know I say that a lot but I'm writing this while munching on a salad
drizzled with this dressing. It's sweet and sour and the texture is so creamy,
which all makes it great on any burger or salad.*

Sometimes when I teach how to make this in my online cooking classes people go:

Oh, I just want to swim in it. It's that delicious!

Ingredients

1 cup cashew nuts, soaked for an hour and rinsed well
1 small shallot, peeled
1/2 tsp turmeric powder
1/4 cup apple cider vinegar
1/4 cup coconut sugar or dates
3/4 cup water
3 tbsp yellow mustard
Salt and black pepper, to taste
1 cup #LOVE

Method

Add the ingredients to a blender and blend until smooth.

Taste and season if needed.

Store in a jar. It keeps in the fridge for 3 days.

PREP TIME 5-8 mins
FREEZER-FRIENDLY No
R, RSF

MAKES 450 ML

Creamy Leek Sauce

*I learned about this incredible sauce back in 2005 when I worked in a health retreat.
What a great recipe! It's creamy, delicious and lovely on any steamed veggies.
It can also be served with any roast dinner as a sauce on the side. It's actually
so versatile that I used it as a cheesy pasta sauce in mac and cheese, and so on.*

*I love the fact that I have this opportunity to share the recipe with you.
It's such a simple recipe yet it's a game changer as it can be used as a replacement for cream.
And that's what this is all about: making smart food choices.*

Ingredients

1 leek, including the green
part, sliced into rings
3 cups water
1 cup cashew nuts
1 garlic clove
Salt and black pepper, to
taste
1 Tbsp #POSITIVITY

Method

Add the ingredients to a pot and bring to the boil.

Reduce the heat to a low simmer and cook for 10 more
minutes.

Turn off the heat and let it rest.

Transfer to your blender and blend until creamy and
completely smooth.

Taste and adjust the seasoning if needed.

Enjoy over steamed veggies.

PREP TIME 5 mins
COOKING TIME 15 mins
FREEZER-FRIENDLY No
R, RSF

MAKES 500 ML

Caesar Dressing

This is the Caesar of all Caesars. I created it out of the blue at my friend's house a few weeks back on a lazy Sunday. It all started with the classic question: What's for lunch? I'm hungry.

I opened her fridge and besides one half empty jar of My Pro-B+ there was a bag of organic lettuce. Still alive and fresh but oh so very lonely...

I needed something to enrich the lettuce with flavour, and luckily I had the support of my friend:

You're genius mate, I'm sure you will figure it out, Cyn.

One lettuce, some toasted bread, and this glorious dressing later we were enjoying one of the best Caesar salads I've ever eaten. Hail Caesar!

Ingredients

1/2 cup cashews
1 tsp dijon mustard
2-3 tbsp savoury yeast
1 garlic clove, smashed
2 shallots
200ml Kara coconut cream
1 tbsp apple cider vinegar
1 tbsp maple syrup
A pinch of salt
A pinch of black pepper
1 cup #TRUST

Method

Add all the ingredients to a blender and blend until smooth.

PREP TIME 10 mins
FREEZER-FRIENDLY No
R, RSF

MAKES 300 ML

I've come up with this little situation of glory.

Tahini Orange Dressing

I was taught to make this dressing by the wonderful and extremely talented Chef Diogo. For years, I was starving for a Chef in my life; one that will share openly without fear, who feels the true essence of respecting food cultures around the world and recreates those dishes into something that the body understands.

Now I want to pass this recipe to you. The recipe is also included in my online cooking classes and there I show how I like to use it – I spread a generous amount on my Lighten UP bread, top it with roasted veggies, sprinkle with some chopped garlic, salt and pepper and give it just a drizzle of olive oil. The combo of flavours is stunning.

Ingredients

300ml orange juice
1 1/2 tbsp tamari
1/4 cup tahini
1 tbsp #PATIENCE

Method

Preheat a pot on high and then pour in the orange juice and tamari.

Boil until the mixture turns into a syrup.

Remove from the heat and stir in the tahini. If needed, add a little water to make a thick paste.

PREP TIME 3 mins
COOKING TIME 10 mins
FREEZER-FRIENDLY No
R, RSF, NF

MAKES 200 ML

Satay Sauce

I developed this sauce years ago after living in Indonesia. It has a nice umami flavour coming through the savoury flavour of the sesame seed oil and the sweet and salty playfulness of tamari. The heat of the chilli ramps up the incredible taste of this satay sauce.

You can pair it with any buddha bowl or just put it there on the table and use it as a condiment. I tried it with noodles and as a stir-fry sauce and it's amazing. I especially love the depth of flavour it gives to raw dishes.

Ingredients

1/2 cup almond butter
1/3 cup raw cashews
2 1/2cm slice of fresh ginger
A pinch of cayenne
1 small garlic clove
1 tbsp sesame oil
2 tbsp tamari
2 tbsp maple syrup, or coconut sugar
1 cup water
Salt and black pepper, to taste
1 Tbsp #ABUNDANCE

Method

Add all the ingredients to your blender and blend until creamy.

Serve with your favourite buddha bowl and enjoy!

PREP TIME 5-8 mins
FREEZER-FRIENDLY No
C, RSF

MAKES: 450 ML

Nacho Cheese Sauce

The only way for you to know how epic this rich, thick and cheesy sauce is, is to make it. I use it as a dip, drizzled over nachos, in my mac and cheese, in a veggie bake, as a pizza cheese, the list goes on and on. Sometimes I just park myself on the couch with a bowl of corn chips and a jar of this glorious sauce. It's my version of a tasty heaven.

Ingredients

200g carrots, unpeeled and cut into large chunks
300g potato, peeled and cut into large chunks
160g raw cashews
2 garlic cloves, smashed
1/2 onion, roughly chopped
1 tsp turmeric powder
1l water
1 1/2 tsp dijon mustard
1/4 cup savoury yeast, or to taste
1 tsp salt
A pinch of black pepper
A pinch of #INSPIRATION

Method

Add the first 7 ingredients to a medium-size pot and bring to the boil.

Turn down the heat to a medium simmer and cook for 40 minutes or until the ingredients are completely soft.

Turn off the heat and allow to rest for 10 minutes in the pot.

Drain the veggies and reserve the cooking water.

Put the veggies into a blender, add the mustard and savoury yeast, and blend on high speed until smooth and creamy. If you'd like the sauce to be thinner, add more cooking water.

Taste and adjust the seasonings if needed.

PREP TIME 5 mins
COOKING TIME 30-40 mins
FREEZER-FRIENDLY Yes
C, RSF

SERVES 4

Balsamic Glaze

Balsamic glaze is like every chef's dream, you know? I love it, too! It's such a beautiful fusion of flavours – sweet, tangy, and acidic. It's one of those incredible condiments that just sit there and you don't even have to put it in the fridge. It's as if it belongs to your kitchen shelf and lasts forever; I'm talking like 12 months.

It is very versatile too. I use it as a condiment when I have scrambled tofu for breakfast or when I have friends visiting me in my studio. I put some sourdough bread, olive oil, my balsamic glaze, and salt on the table and everyone gathers around and enjoys. Then the questions start:

Why is your balsamic so much better than mine?

It's glazed. And... it's made with coconut sugar, not processed white sugar.

Enjoy enjoy enjoy.

Ingredients

460ml balsamic vinegar
2 cups coconut sugar
1 tbsp #COMFORT

Method

Add the ingredients to a small pot and bring to the boil.

Reduce the heat to simmer and start your timer for 20 minutes.

When done, allow to cool and then transfer to a sauce bottle.

COOKING TIME 20 mins
FREEZER-FRIENDLY No
C, RSF, NF

MAKES 200 ML

Sour Cream

All you dairy-free people out there who love dairy but cannot have it, here is an amazing alternative for sour cream. It is simple and easy to make, full of healthy fats and freaking delicious. I created this recipe a long time ago for my friends Courtney and Michelle. They both can't have dairy because they get weird coughing and sneezing fits, but this dairy-free sour cream is the best alternative to the store-bought sour cream I have ever come across.

It mimics the texture of the conventional sour cream, it is really white, and the taste is epic. This is real goodness and since it is rich in plant fats you don't have to worry because it will serve your body well.

There are so many ways to use this glory. You can have it as a dip with corn chips, wraps or on top of whole, roasted spuds or sweet potatoes.

Ingredients

1 1/2 cup cashew nuts, soaked 4-8 hours or over night, in 3 cups of water, drained and rinsed well
1 lime, juiced
1 lemon, juiced
1/2 cup water
1/2 tsp salt
1 tbsp #FAITH

Method

Add the ingredients to your blender and blend until very smooth and creamy.

PREP TIME 2-3 mins
FREEZER-FRIENDLY No
R, RSF

MAKES 200 ML

Hoisin Sauce

When I was trying to make this, I thought:

"Cynthia, you know you can buy hoisin sauce everywhere. You will never be able to make it the same as a store-bought hoisin sauce."

Well, that was me talking to myself and then discovering that I actually didn't want it to be the same as the store-bought sauce.

I was after something different. Something that's full of flavour and gets even better as days go by. With all of these wholefood recipes we try to create flavour from nature, and that's why this sauce is so amazing. It's also incredible when mixed with a little bit of coconut milk and turned into a dipping sauce. If you add a couple of drops of smokey liquid it transforms into a lovely BBQ sauce to drizzle over tacos.

Ingredients

4 tbsp tamari
2 tsp tahini
2 garlic cloves, grated
2 tbsp tomato puree
4 tbsp coconut sugar
2 tbsp apple cider vinegar
A pinch of dried chili
3ml #FORGIVENESS

Method

Add the ingredients to a small pot and simmer for 5 minutes.

Stir continuously to prevent burning.

Keep in the fridge for up to 10 days.

COOKING TIME 5-8 mins
FREEZER-FRIENDLY Yes
R, RSF, NF

MAKES 125ML

Maple Mustard Dressing

*My son Jayman used to buy Subway and get the honey mustard dressing with it.
These types of store-bought dressings are full of flavous but also full of numbers
(yes, numbers are for counting, not for eating). Real flavour comes from
nature and not food labs. So I created my version of honey mustard dressing
for my son and all of you out there.*

*Clearly, I used maple. If you are using honey, keep in mind the type of honey.
If you stay away from fragrant honey and stick with a more neutral one, all the flavours
will settle together into an incredible dressing. It keeps well in a glass bottle
or jar for week. Use it on whatever you like, not just salads.*

Ingredients

1/4 cup dijon mustard

1/4 cup maple syrup

1 tbsp apple cider vinegar

1/4 cup olive oil

5g onion, finely diced

1 garlic clove

2 tbsp lemon juice

2 tbsp water

Salt and black pepper, to taste

A pinch of #RESPECT

Method

Add all the ingredients to your blender and blend until creamy, thick and smooth.

PREP TIME 2-3 mins
FREEZER-FRIENDLY No
R, RSF, NF

MAKES 200 ML

Tzatziki

The story of this recipe goes back to a fasting retreat, which may sound like an odd place to create a recipe but let me tell you, the role of a chef in a fasting retreat is one of the things I value the most about my job. Not only do I teach people how to break the fast but also how to continue the healing process after they leave the retreat.

Life out there is not easy. We need to stay strong and make wise lifestyle choices, so my job is to bring ease to this space. I do this by inspiring, educating, and allowing the transformation to happen with ease and flow. This tzatziki recipe is a perfect example of how that transformation can happen without stress.

It was the morning of the 10th day of fasting. Imagine drinking only juice for 10 days and feeling how your body is going through detox. When you see a freshly made wholefood meal, your body perks up, all your senses wake up and you are overwhelmed with appreciation. Witnessing this is epic!

Anyways, I was demonstrating how to make this dairy-free tzatziki and everyone was allowed to taste a tiny bit. There was one beautiful soul in the group, who, overwhelmed with joy, said:

I'm Greek, Chef and ever since my childhood I couldn't have any dairy. I've been dreaming of my grandmother's tzatziki. I can't believe how close this is to the original. I'm floored! I love you Chef!

It's these stories and food memories that make my heart shine, and I trust that some of you or someone you know have been craving for a scoop of dairy-free tzatziki, too.

Tag me on social media when they discover my tzatziki; I want to see that joy!

Ingredients

One portion of my sour
cream recipe
1 cup grated cucumber
1/2 cup mint, finely chopped
Salt and black pepper,
to taste
1 cup #EASE & FLOW

Method

Squeeze out and discard all the cucumber liquid.

Mix together all the ingredients and serve.

PREP TIME 5 mins
FREEZER-FRIENDLY No
R, RSF

MAKES 250 ML

Green Ranch

Ranch dressing was something I hadn't known about until an American friend of mine said:

Oh, you should do ranch dressing.

I was like What's that? and after I got my explanation, I made it.

My biggest challenge for this recipe was to recreate the same zing, sweetness, texture, and full flavour using wholefood ingredients. The final result is delicious, can go with anything, and stores well in the fridge for up to 5 days.

Ingredients

1 cup cashew nuts, soaked overnight in 2 cups of water, drained and rinsed well
1 tbsp apple cider vinegar
1 cup fresh basil leaves
1/2 cup fresh dill
1 garlic clove
1/2 lemon, juiced
3/4 cup water
2 tbsp maple syrup
Salt and black pepper, to taste
20ml #GRATITUDE

Method

Add the ingredients to your blender and blend until smooth and creamy.

PREP TIME 2-3 mins
COOKING TIME 5 mins
FREEZER-FRIENDLY No
R, RSF

MAKES 250 ML

Smokey BBQ Sauce

This smokey BBQ sauce is based on my hoisin sauce. Basically I just added a couple of drops of liquid smoke to the hoisin sauce and voila. It's the perfect replacement for store-bought BBQ sauce, which is usually loaded with rubbish and white sugar.

Ingredients

4 tbsp tamari
4 tsp tahini
2 garlic cloves, grated
2 tbsp tomato puree
4 tbsp coconut sugar
2 tbsp apple cider vinegar
4-5 drops of liquid smoke
A pinch of dried chili
A pinch of #PEACE

COOKING TIME 5-8 mins
FREEZER-FRIENDLY Yes
R, RSF, NF

Method

Add the ingredients to a small pot and simmer for 5 minutes.

Stir continuously to prevent burning.

Store in the fridge for up to 10 days.

MAKES 125ML

Togarashi Sauce

A lovely bit of flavour for a dipping sauce or with noodles in a stir fry.

Ingredients

3 tbsp tamari
1 tbsp maple syrup
1 tbsp sesame oil
1 tsp grated ginger
A pinch of cayenne pepper
1 tbsp #ACCEPTANCE

Method

Whisk together all the ingredients until combined.

Drizzle generously over steamed veggies or rice and enjoy!

PREP TIME 2 mins
FREEZER-FRIENDLY No
R, RSF, NF

MAKES 1/3 CUP

Invest in your inner health contract using real ingredients.

Cold Liquids

Our minds have allowed us to develop civilization, create incredible technology, and change the face of our planet. One thing that never changes is our desire to eat, to nourish ourselves, and to share that food and nourishment with others.

Enjoy these cold liquids on a hot day. They taste even better with a friend.

Turmeric Spritzer

*Have you heard of jamu? It's a traditional Indonesian drink that is so glorious
it's even considered a medicine. In essence jamu is made from fresh turmeric, lime, and honey.
Turmeric gives jamu its vibrant, orange colour and also turns it into a incredibly powerful
anti-inflammatory drink.*

*Jamu has been enjoyed for centuries and is an integral part of Indonesian life.
Some people experiment in order to enhance the flavour of jamu – one of my friends
adds aloe vera and black pepper, other people add lemongrass or ginger.
It may sound like a weird combination, but it's pretty tasty actually.*

*I've added my own twist to the traditional jamu recipe and turned it into a jamu spritzer!
Now get all up in it!*

*The signature flavour is still there but now – wait for it – as opposed to the original jamu
(which is very concentrate), my spritzer version is lighter and sparkly and looks like a cocktail!*

You can thank me now or you can thank me later ;)

Ingredients

200g fresh turmeric, juiced
1 lime, skin removed, juiced
Maple syrup, as much as
you like
Soda water, as needed
Ice, for serving
A pinch of #COURAGE

Method

Mix the turmeric and lime juice with the maple syrup.

Fill the glasses with ice, pour an equal amount of the
turmeric mix into two glasses and top with soda water.

PREP TIME 5 mins
FREEZER-FRIENDLY No
R, RSF, NF

SERVES 2

Green Slushy

I love herbs and include them in my meals as much as I can, so it's no surprise that this slushy recipe is packed with parsley power. Let me tell you this – it may seem like an unusual combination but the flavours are so well balanced I'm sure you will enjoy this drink even if you are not a fan of parsley.

How do you balance flavours? Well that's my job. Yours is to drink the sh*t out of this awe-inspiring drink... Its green colour is so lush and inviting you won't be able to resist.

Ingredients

3 limes, juiced
1 cup flat-leaf parsley, packed tightly
1 cup water
Maple syrup, as much as you like
1 tray of ice
1 cup #RESPECT

Method

Add all the ingredients to the blender and blend until combined and resembles an icy slush of glory.

Serve and enjoy!

PREP TIME 5 mins
FREEZER-FRIENDLY No
R, RSF, NF

SERVES 1

Master Cleanse

*This master cleanse is the best way to start your day.
Its lemony power wakes you up, the maple syrup balances you out and
makes this tasty beverage mellow enough not to throw you into shock.*

I love adding just a bit of cayenne pepper to give a warm hug to my organs.

This is a wonderful, wonderful drink. Enjoy it and express #gratitude.

Ingredients

2-3 lemons, juiced
750ml water
1/4 tsp or more cayenne pepper
1/4 cup maple syrup*
A pinch of salt
Lots of ice
A pinch of #ACCEPTANCE

*You can adjust the amount of maple syrup to your taste

Method

Add all the ingredients to a large jar, seal and shake to combine.

Enjoy!

PREP TIME 5 mins
FREEZER-FRIENDLY No
R, RSF, NF

SERVES 1

Coriander & Pineapple

My best combo to date! Nothing to add here other than to say make it Fresh!
Fresh pineapple. Fresh coriander. Nothing more. Nothing less. Enjoy!

Ingredients

500ml freshly juiced
pineapple
70ml freshly juiced
coriander
Lots of ice
1 cup #PATIENCE

Method

Add the ingredients to the blender and blend until combined.

Fill the glasses with ice and top with your detox drink.

Serve and enjoy each sip of this epic drink!

PREP TIME 5 mins
FREEZER-FRIENDLY No
R, RSF, NF

SERVES 2

Carrot & Ginger Fizz

This recipe is a guide to expand what's possible with simple juices.
Add ginger and sweetener to suit your taste. Just try it first before you decide
how much maple syrup to add – some carrots are sweeter than others.

Ingredients

400ml fresh carrot juice
1 lemon, juiced
2 1/2cm of ginger root,
minced
1-2 tbsp maple syrup
1 can soda water
Lots of ice
A pinch of #SELFWORTH

Method

Add the carrot and lemon juice, ginger, maple syrup,
and a handful of ice to your blender and blend to combine.

Fill your glasses with ice, divide the carrot and ginger mix
equally and top with the soda water.

PREP TIME 5 mins
FREEZER-FRIENDLY No
R, RSF, NF

SERVES 2

Hello Liver, meet Cucumber.

Black Lemonade

Great for parties. Halloween, and a simple drink to turn heads!
Find your own way with this drink. There's a balance between the ratio
of lemon and sweetener which you can rediscover every time.

Ingredients

1 lemon, juiced
Maple syrup, as much as
you like
1/4 tsp activated charcoal,
add more if you like
1 can soda water
Ice, for serving
A pinch of #TRUST

Method

Add the lemon juice, maple syrup, and charcoal to a jar,
seal and shake to combine.

Divide equally into 3 glasses, top with soda water and drink!

PREP TIME 2 mins
FREEZER-FRIENDLY No
R, RSF, NF

SERVES 3

Cucumber Cleanser

This cucumber cleanser reminds me of my mate Christina and one interesting thing she does. I noticed this for the first time many months ago while we were eating together in our café: she requested more cucumbers in her salad.

This became a regular thing for Christina and it got me thinking how our bodies gravitate towards certain ingredients over time.

Hence my inspiration to create a simple, refreshing drink providing our bodies with much needed hydration.

Besides cucumbers, salt plays an important role in this recipe because it enhances the cucumber flavour. Cucumber cleanser is now one of my fav drinks on a hot day.

We'll leave the last word to Christina: "Oh, yeah, I like it!"

Ingredients

1 cucumber, sliced thinly
Lots of ice
3 cucumbers, juiced
A pinch of salt
A pinch of #FORGIVENESS

Method

Add the sliced cucumber to your serving glasses and top with ice.

Mix the cucumber juice with some salt and pour into the glasses.

PREP TIME 5 mins
FREEZER-FRIENDLY No
R, RSF, NF

MAKES 1 LITRE

Parsley & Pineapple

This is the most perfect detox drink I have ever tasted in my life.
Period. The End. Full stop.

I had it in LA years ago and I'm filled with happiness to share this with you.
It's refreshing, loaded with iron and vitamin C and the colour is amazing.
It makes you want to drink it straight from your blender.
Actually you should do exactly that. Drink it straight from the damn blender.
Then tell me about it. Your liver loves you just for reading this.

Ingredients

500ml freshly juiced
pineapple (1 pineapple)
200ml fresh parsley juice (2
bunches of flat-leaf parsley)
Ice, for serving
A pinch of
#CONTENTMENT

Method

Add the pineapple and parsley juice into the blender and blend for 5 seconds pour into the glasses filled with ice.

Treat yourself with a glass of this glorious drink!

PREP TIME 5 mins
FREEZER-FRIENDLY No
R, RSF, NF

SERVES 2

Ways to my heart
1. Buy me food
2. Make me food
3. Be food.

Lunch

Real food makes you feel good
after you eat it.

I've learnt that the closer to nature it is,
and the less human interference it has,
the better it is for you.

When I choose ingredients like this and
cook them with thoughts and feelings
like #gratitude, #joy, #lettinggo, #love,
#courage, something magical happens
to my body and my mind.

Now that's the way to do lunch.

Caesar Salad

*It was a sunny Sunday in Bali around 1pm and I was at my mate's house.
Kids were having fun at the pool and my mate Rachelle suddenly decided she was hungry!
The last thing I wanted was to go to the store, but the situation didn't look promising.*

*Rachelle is a person who likes order and system, so finding ingredients that I wanted would
be like sifting gold in a silver mine! To make things even more challenging, Rachelle doesn't
cook! As in ever. She is one of those people who are great at big picture visioning, so she
helps humanity in her way and leaves cooking to other genius human around her.*

*So I had to work with what I had while keeping in mind that Rachelle loves a bit of crunch
in her food. Rachelle pulled up a chair to keep me company and I started hunting for
ingredients. As I saw some random slices of sourdough bread and a lonely iceberg lettuce,
I knew exactly what I wanted to make.*

*Moments later I'm preparing homemade croutons that turned out
super crunchy and golden brown.*

*Then came the epic moment of preparing plant-based Caesar dressing.
We ended up having a creamy, cheesy dressing where sour and sweet flavours dance
together in a perfect unison. I tried my best to remember all the isms I used on that day
and since then this salad has been a regular visitor on my dining table.
I hope you'll enjoy this magnificent dish too!*

Ingredients

FOR THE CROUTONS:

A generous splash of olive
oil
A pinch of salt
3 slices GF sourdough
bread, cut into cubes

FOR ASSEMBLING:

1 large iceberg lettuce,
roughly chopped
Caesar dressing, as much as
you like
1 tbsp #CONTENTMENT

Method

To prepare the croutons:

Pour the oil in a pan, sprinkle with a pinch of salt
and add the bread cubes.

Give it a stir to coat the cubes with the oil and leave
to fry on medium-high heat.

Stir from time to time to avoid burning.

When done, transfer to a paper towel to drain.

To serve:

Drizzle the iceberg lettuce with the Caesar dressing,
top with the croutons and serve!

PREP TIME 10 mins
FREEZER-FRIENDLY No
C, RSF

SERVES 1-2

Burger Patty

Veggie patties, in my opinion, are normally dry, bland and simply full of rice, chickpeas or black beans. Not that there's anything wrong with those ingredients – it's just too much when you've worked all day and just want to smash something together fast.

I think of all the mums, dads, grandparents and singles out there doing the best they can with what they have in the fridge. This recipe is for all of us. It's fast, can be served as a burger, as a rissole with my yummy gravy, or with salad and my homemade tomato sauce. Whatever you decide to do, I trust you will find this moment to reflect on how wonderful you are. I dedicate this recipe to you and your family.

Ingredients

1/2 leek, thinly sliced
4 garlic cloves, roughly chopped
150g button mushrooms
2 medium carrots, grated
1 cup fresh basil leaves, packed tightly
1 tbsp dried oregano
1/2 cup fresh parsley, packed tightly
1 1/2 cup breadcrumbs
2 tbsp psyllium husk
1/2 cup cassava flour
Salt and black pepper, to taste
A pinch of #LOVE

Method

Add the ingredients to your food processor except the cassava flour, psyllium husk, and breadcrumbs.

Process well until combined but make sure to leave a bit of texture.

Transfer to a bowl, add the remaining ingredients and mix well.

Take half of the mixture, add it back to the food processor and blend well.

Return the mixture back to the bowl and combine.

Roll the mixture into patties (around 140 grams each), toss in some breadcrumbs and leave to rest for 5-8 minutes.

Heat some coconut oil on a grill or in a pan on medium heat.

Cook the patties until golden brown and serve with my coleslaw salad.

PREP TIME 10-15 mins
COOKING TIME 15-20 mins
FREEZER-FRIENDLY Yes
C, RSF, NF

MAKES 6 PATTIES

Satay Veggies

Every time and I mean every time I demo this on stage for the past 8 years it flips people out. They become born-again-satay-sauce-eaters. Noble, satay cult followers. Believers of a new way of satay.

The husbands in the audience that were dragged to the event can't believe that the hippy chef (me) made something that tasted so damn good. And it becomes the new normal on the menu in homes around the globe...

That's when I know that I've done my job well.

Ingredients

FOR THE VEGGIES:

1 carrot, shredded
5 long beans, sliced into
bite-size pieces*
1 cup mung bean sprouts
1/2 cucumber, cut into thin strips
1/2 capsicum, cut into thin strips
3 spring onions, sliced into rings
1 corn cob, kernels removed
1 cup coriander, tightly packed
and roughly chopped
1 cup Vietnamese mint leaves
Salt and black pepper, to taste
1 tbsp #FORGIVENESS
*Can be substituted with snow
peas or any other beans

FOR THE DRESSING:

1/2 cup almond butter
1/3 cup raw cashews
2 1/2cm slice fresh ginger
or more if you like
A pinch of cayenne pepper
1 small garlic clove
1 tbsp sesame oil
2 tbsp tamari
2 tbsp maple syrup or
coconut sugar
1 cup water
Salt and black pepper, to taste

Method

To prepare the veggies:

Add all the veggie ingredients to a bowl, season well and set aside.

To prepare the dressing:

Add the ingredients to your Vitamix and blend until smooth and creamy.

Taste and adjust the seasonings if needed.

Flood the veggies with the dressing and toss to combine.

Serve and enjoy!

PREP TIME 10-15 mins
FREEZER-FRIENDLY No
R, *NF, RSF
*NF – does not refer to the almond dressing

450ML OF DRESSING
SERVES: 2

I don't believe in one "ism"...
Just cook as nature intended.

Green Machine Fritters

Create a breakfast menu, Chef, today. Like NOW!

This is what Simone, my partner in one of the many cafés we have built together declared in one of our team meetings.

I was like RightO, mate... RightO!!! (Read this in my Aussie accent).

Anyhoo, these babies are a joy to eat, they make everything in the fritter world so much better. Serve them with wild rocket, cherry tomatoes, my raita and a splash of my balsamic glaze. They will become a staple in your house and you I guarantee you'll just eat them all the time.

Bless Simone for believing in me. I love working with her. Fun fact about my mate Sim: her profile on the Wealth Dynamic Test is a Mechanic (Wealth Dynamics is a system invented by my mate Roger Hamilton which tells you the exact strategy you should follow to build wealth).

Mechanics can quietly think in their own corner, taking apart and putting together things that already exist. As a result, what they build is built to last. As endless perfectionists, Mechanics will keep finding ways to improve systems and processes, making things simple and smart. That's who Mechanics are, no matter what type of service they deliver – be it app development or burgers.

Simone is my Guru. When I get stuck trying to figure it all out, she is there with an answer, and in her calm and clever way, she brings order to chaos. That's why we work so well together!

Ingredients

Olive oil, for cooking
340g onions, finely diced
30g garlic, finely diced
100g celery, chopped
200g broccoli, sliced thinly
360g zucchini, grated
220g spinach, sliced
100g spring onions, finely
sliced
1/2 bunch fresh parsley
80g gluten-free flour
Salt and black pepper, to
taste
1 cup #ABUNDANCE

Method

Pour the olive oil in a large pot and heat on medium heat.

Add the onions, garlic, celery, and broccoli and season with salt and pepper.

Sauté for 5 minutes but do not brown the veggies.

Add the zucchini and sauté for 3 more minutes.

Stir in the spinach, spring onions, and parsley and sauté for 1 more minute.

Leave the mixture to cool down.

Squeeze out and discard the liquid from the cooked veggies and herbs.

Add the flour and mix to combine.

Add coconut oil to a hot plate and pour 1/3 cup of the patty mixture at a time.

Cook for about 10 minutes, depending on how thick patties are. Do not press the patties down while cooking.

Serve warm and enjoy!

PREP TIME 10 mins
COOKING TIME 8-12 mins
FREEZER-FRIENDLY No
C, NF, RSF

6 LARGE PATTIES

Potato Salad & Cultured Yogurt Dressing

This is a cool dish, and although it looks basic, it's super yum.
The key here is to choose small potatoes. I tried out this recipe with big spuds
but they just don't make the cut.

Showering beautiful, steamed little potatoes with fresh dill, mint
or any other herbs makes the dish stunning and adds so much flavour.
Go ahead, make it and enjoy it for lunch or dinner.

Ingredients

500g baby potatoes,
unpeeled

My anti-inflammatory
dressing, for serving

Shallots, as much as you
like, thinly sliced

Spring onions, as much as
you like, thinly sliced

Fresh dill, as much as you
like

Fresh mint, as much as you
like

A pinch of #TRUST

Method

Steam the potatoes until cooked through.

Leave to cool down, drizzle with the dressing
and top with the shallots, spring onions, and herbs.

Toss to combine, take a deep breath and treat
yourself with this epic salad!

PREP TIME 2-3 mins
(COOKING TIME 20-30 mins
FREEZER-FRIENDLY No
C, RSF

SERVES 2

Rainbow Rolls

*You either can roll these or you can't. These can be painful at times, so ya gotta be quick.
One tip is to dip the rice paper in cold water (not hot) so they become easier to handle.
Also, don't let them soak in the water too long or they get soggy. Work with one at a time,
allowing it to go into the water just a bit and start rolling while the paper is still firm.*

*One more thing; put whatever you like in them. Once I used leftover rice, lettuce and herbs
and they turned out just fine. Be free with this recipe and keep the pressure of rolling away.*

*If you truly suck at rolling, leave the rice paper out and make a deconstructed bowl.
Basically, it will be a giant salad and you can use rice noodles to add the texture.*

Ingredients

FOR THE FILLING*

1/4 red capsicum,
thinly sliced
1 carrot, thinly sliced
1 lettuce, thinly sliced
1 cucumber, thinly sliced
A handful of mint leaves
A handful of coriander
leaves
1 packet of tempeh,
sliced and grilled
Salt and black pepper,
to taste
1 cup of #JOY
*You can use any veggies
and herbs of your choice

FOR THE ASSEMBLY:

1 packet of rice paper
rounds (22cm)

FOR THE DRESSING:

2 tbsp sesame seed oil
2 tbsp tamari
2 tbsp umeboshi plum
vinegar
1/2 tbsp tahini
2 tbsp maple syrup
1 tbsp ginger, grated
1 green chili, thinly sliced

PREP TIME 20 mins
FREEZER-FRIENDLY No
C, GF, NF

Method

TO PREPARE THE ROLLS:

Season all the raw ingredients with salt and pepper.

Fill a shallow tray with water at room temperature.

Dip a rice paper round in the tray and keep it there
for 15 seconds or until just soft.

Place the paper on a flat surface and add the filling
ingredients to the middle of the paper.

Fold in the ends and roll up the paper firmly to enclose
the filling.

Repeat the same with the remaining rice papers
and fillings.

TO PREPARE THE DRESSING:

Whisk together the ingredients until well combined.

Serve with your rainbow rolls.

SERVES 6-8

Green Quinoa Patties

I highly recommend serving this one with my tzatziki recipe. Load it up with fresh salad and finish it with my balsamic glaze. Now you're a chef! BOOM!!

Really, the complete combo I just mentioned works. Every mouthful will be packed with flavour, and if you have leftovers they will still be epic the next day.

Ingredients

1 cup raw quinoa

2 cups of water

2 garlic cloves, smashed

1/2 tsp coriander powder

2 cups cooked green peas

2 tbsp ground flax seeds

2 tbsp gluten-free flour

1/4 cup spring onions, finely chopped

1/4 cup fresh parsley, roughly chopped

Salt, to taste

Coconut oil, for frying

1 portion of my tzatziki, for serving

1 cup #PEACE

Method

Add the quinoa, water, and garlic to a rice cooker, season with salt and press Play.

Add the cooked green peas, cooked quinoa, herbs, spices, flax, flour and seasoning to a food processor and pulse until combined, allowing for some texture.

Allow the mixture to rest for 5 minutes.

Divide the mixture into 7-8 equal parts and form patties.

Heat a pan on medium-high and add coconut oil.

Cook the patties for 2-3 minutes on both sides or until golden brown.

Top the patties with the garnish and a generous dollop of tzatziki and serve immediately.

PREP TIME 5 mins
COOKING TIME 5 mins
FREEZER-FRIENDLY No
C, RSF, NF

SERVES 4

Together we're better.

Fast Nachos

Ping!! My phone goes off, as it does all day, with epic messages from lovely fans and friends. This ping was from my friend Hayley, announcing she had made the best yellow cheese sauce she had ever tasted. She continued on and ended the message with

It just needs the Chef Cynthia Louise magic.
Basically, make it more epic.

Challenge accepted!!

This sauce has changed so many lives. It turned people into confident cooks who now make this recipe at least once a week. It's helped mums around the world with kids who are intolerant to dairy and who now can enjoy nachos. It's been a life-changing sauce for older kids heading to the college or moving out and craving fast, go-to recipes they can afford. It has brought absolute joy to new cooks who thought that the only way to have a cheesy, creamy sauce like this is to use cheese.

It's without a doubt a life-saving recipe, and thanks to Hayley we all get to dive deep into its epicness. Use it as a dip, over nachos, for mac and cheese or pour it hot over steamed veggies.

Ingredients

1 fresh corn cob, kernels removed

2 ripe tomatoes, chopped into bite-size pieces

A handful of fresh coriander, roughly chopped

2 spring onions, thinly sliced

1/4 cup sliced jalapenos

1 red long chili, sliced into rings

Salt and black pepper, to taste

1 lime, juiced

GMO-free corn chips, as much as you want

2 portions of my nacho cheese sauce

A pinch of #SELFWORTH

Method

Add all the ingredients except the lime juice, corn chips and cheese sauce to a bowl and mix to combine.

Season with salt and pepper and drizzle with the lime juice.

Top your corn chips with this mix and shower with the nacho cheese sauce.

PREP TIME 15 mins
COOKING TIME 30-40 mins (for the cheese sauce)
FREEZER-FRIENDLY Yes, the cheese is freezer-friendly
C, RSF

SERVES 4-6

Donna's Veggie Balls

Where do I start... Well, my mate Donna is a fantastic cook, like a proper one that explores and gives recipes a good hard crack. These balls needed a name and to come up with a proper name to match the moments in the kitchen with Donna is unfortunately impossible.

While you're here, make a note that sometimes the teriyaki sauce feels like there's not enough of it, so be sure you don't reduce it too much as it evaporates away into space. Can't have that now, can we?

How do you serve 'em and eat 'em? Well, for Donna and me, it's straight out of the pan into a puddle of sauce. We then stand back, wait for a bit, like 10 minutes and then we attack them! Grab and swish them around the sauce and from there right into the mouth. That's it, nothing more, nothing less. They are an excellent little add-on to one's life. Don't believe me? Try them out!

Ingredients

FOR THE HOMEMADE TERIYAKI SAUCE:

3 tsp grated ginger
2 tsp maple syrup
1/4 cup tamari
1/4 cup apple cider vinegar
1/4 cup water

FOR THE BALLS:

200g eggplant, chopped into bite-sized chunks
1 cup rice, cooked
1 spring onion, thinly sliced
1 garlic clove, grated
2cm ginger, grated
1/2 tsp sesame seed oil
1 tsp tamari
1/2 cup breadcrumbs
2 tsp psyllium
A handful of fresh coriander, chopped roughly, for garnishing
1 tbsp #LETTINGGO

Method

To prepare the sauce:

Add the ingredients to a small pot and cook until the liquid thickens and reduces a little. Set aside.

To prepare the balls:

Add the eggplant to a small pan and pour in enough water to cover the eggplant.

Bring to the boil and cook until soft and the water has evaporated.

Drain the eggplant well. Transfer to a food processor, add the rice, spring onion, garlic, ginger, sesame seed oil, and tamari and blend until the ingredients are combined, allowing a little texture.

Transfer the mixture to a bowl and mix in the breadcrumbs and psyllium.

Roll the mixture into small balls (around 40 grams) and place them in the fridge for 30 minutes to set.

Fry the balls until brown.

Serve with the teriyaki sauce and garnished with coriander.

PREP TIME 10 mins
COOKING TIME 10 mins
FREEZER-FRIENDLY Yes
C, RSF, NF

SERVES 3-4

Raw Broccoli Salad

This is yet another recipe that's a game-changer, especially if you're on a raw food healing program. The key thing to nail with this beautiful dish is to cut the broccoli into really tiny florets. There is nothing worse than big bite-size chunks of raw broccoli – yerch – so for my sake alone please cut them small.

This is a great recipe to use your hands. Massage the veggies with the sauce. If you're a no-hands-in-food human then use any tool to get it all well combined and don't forget to bless those hands using the tools. Your hands are fantastic (just like you) and who knows what life would be like without them. Right?

Ingredients

FOR THE DRESSING:

2 tbsp tamari
2 tbsp sesame oil
1 tbsp maple syrup
1/4 cup sesame seeds
Salt and black pepper, to taste

FOR THE SALAD:

1/2 head of broccoli, divided into bite-sized florets
1/4 red shallot, finely diced
A bunch of spinach or silver beet, chopped into bite-sized pieces
A pinch of #RESPECT

Method

To prepare the dressing:

Whisk together the ingredients and set aside.

To prepare the salad:

Add the ingredients to a bowl, drizzle with the dressing and toss to combine.

Allow to sit for 10 minutes before serving.

PREP TIME 5 mins
FREEZER-FRIENDLY No
R, RSF, NF

SERVES 2-3

Unfried Rice

Whether you're into raw food or not this dish is a beauty.
Unfried rice involves exactly what it sounds like, it's raw and
it's fabulous when you can't be bothered to light the stove.
Over the years I have seen some seriously intense raw recipes
that require dehydrating for long hours or sprouting for days.
I have also eaten some very crappy uncooked meals that are tasteless
and have no soul. This unfried rice is the complete opposite to that.

Here's a big tip for this: the cauliflower must be small. If it's a big one,
cut it in half. If you don't have a food processor, use a grater and make
sure you wring out any moisture in the cauliflower.

Herbs are your friends here; they make the dish
more flavoursome, so add more if you want.

One last thing; the recipe requires your absolute attention
as you mix it with your hands. The true seasoning to any recipe
is your ability to sink into the process of preparing food.
Be present and give your full #ATTENTION and #LOVE
to the ingredients. And of course, rely on your building blocks
of flavour – salt and pepper.

Ingredients

FOR THE BASE:

1 small cauliflower,
roughly chopped
2 spring onions, sliced
1/2 zucchini, small dice
1 yellow capsicum, small dice
1/4 cup fresh coriander,
roughly chopped
1/2 long red chili, sliced
1/2 cup fresh or frozen peas
2 large mushrooms,
thinly sliced
1/3 cup mung bean sprouts
A handful of roasted cashews
or seeds
Salt and black pepper, to taste
1 tbsp #GRATITUDE

FOR THE DRESSING:

3 tbsp tamari
2 tbsp maple syrup
1 tbsp sesame oil
1 tbsp grated ginger
2 tbsp water

PREP TIME 10-15 mins
FREEZER-FRIENDLY No
R, RSF

Method

TO PREPARE THE BASE:

Add the cauliflower to your food processor and pulse for about 5 seconds. Don't overdo it; you need to keep the texture, not turn it into a mash.

Transfer to a large bowl, add the remaining ingredients, season well, stir to combine and set aside.

TO PREPARE THE DRESSING:

Add the ingredients to a small bowl and whisk to combine.

Pour over the cauliflower mixture, mix well and serve.

SERVES 1

Smokey BBQ
Pulled Shroom Burger

I remember the day when I created smokey BBQ sauce. I felt so proud of myself but it was only later that I discovered its full awesomeness. The sauce ended up sitting in the fridge for a couple of days because I didn't know what to pair it with.

But I did have a plan. And the name of that plan was Smokey BBQ Pulled Shrooms.

When the shrooms were ready, I grabbed the sauce from the fridge, tasted it and let me tell you, it was like angels tooting trumpets that's for sure. It was good, like proper good, and not what I expected at all. See, something had happened to the flavour while the sauce was sitting in the fridge. That's the thing when you use real ingredients; they break down, flavours mingle in mysterious ways and get more enhanced. It's cool to witness this magic happen.

Anyhoo, I used organic, salt-reduced tamari by Spiral Foods and I found it to be the key to an epic hoisin sauce, as it's really stable in flavours.

Let me know how this one turns out for you!

Ingredients

Coconut oil, for sautéing
400g oyster mushrooms, pulled into thin strips
3 tbsp smokey BBQ sauce
Salt and black pepper, to taste
1 cup #INSPIRATION

Method

Preheat a pan on medium.

Add a splash of oil and throw in the mushrooms.

Season well and sauté until all the liquid has come out and the mushrooms are looking really charred, stirring as you go.

Pour in the sauce and cook for 1-2 minutes.

Transfer to your burger buns and fill with any salad (or not) that you like.

COOKING TIME 10 mins
FREEZER-FRIENDLY No
C, RSF, NF

SERVES 1-2

Coleslaw with Cultured Coconut Yogurt Dressing

Coleslaw has its own story in Australia. Coleslaw, white bread rolls, and a roast chook is what us, the Aussies, take to the park or beach and enjoy. It's a classic!

You can ask anyone who spent their teenage days in the 90's in Australia and they will for sure say: Oohhh yeah, I remember those days with mum and dad, getting sunburned or suffering from a chest rash from boogie boarding all morning and then being called up from the ocean to join the family and eat. We'd quickly wash our hands, and while the salty ocean water would still be dripping off our bodies, we'd be handed over a white bread roll filled with bits of roast chicken and coleslaw.

That's tradition!

I really hope this recipe ignites your taste buds, floods your hearts with childhood memories and brings a smile to your face. In such moments, all you want to do is pick up your phone and call your mum and dad.

Love you, mum and dad!

Ingredients

FOR THE COLESLAW:

100g red cabbage, shredded
100g green cabbage, shredded
1 carrot, grated
1/2 cup spring onion, sliced
1/4 cup parsley, roughly chopped
1/4 cup sunflower seeds
Salt and black pepper, to taste

FOR THE DRESSING:

1/2 cup cashews, soaked overnight
2 tbsp yellow mustard
2 tsp lemon juice
1/2-1 cup cultured coconut yogurt
3 tbsp maple syrup, optional
Salt and black pepper, to taste
A pinch of #CARE

Method

TO PREPARE THE COLESLAW:

Add all ingredients into a bowl, mix well and set aside.

TO PREPARE THE DRESSING:

Add all to your Vitamix and blend till well combined and smooth.

Combine the coleslaw and the dressing and serve immediately.

PREP TIME 10-15 mins
FREEZER-FRIENDLY No
R, RSF

MAKES: 350ML OF DRESSING
SERVES: 2-3

Remember this moment.

Fresh Chilli Salad

Fresh Chilli Salad is also known as Rincy's Sambal.

Who's Rincy? She's the Balinese nanny to my god-daughter Seaenah and she has the most incredible way of using ingredients.

One day I popped over to see Seaenah and to get to the lounge you have to walk through my favourite part of the house – the kitchen of course. It's where most of the staff hang out and where all sorts of random conversions organically happen.

On that particular day I caught Rincy's eye and thought out loud:

What is on your face?

Leftover lime Chef. It's from the sambal.

Really?

To give you some context, Rincy has the most incredible complexion I have ever seen. She was born and raised in Sumbawa, an island in Indonesia to the east of Bali. For years I would comment on her incredible skin tone and flawless complexion and I would keep pestering her:

What products do you use?

Nothing Chef. Just natural.

Looking back I realise I should have paid more attention to the word Natural.

If I asked "what are the natural things you use" she would have told me all about the limes.

That day as I walked through the kitchen I stopped and spoke to her about the limes – and how the leftover drained limes she uses in the sambal don't make it to the bin until she rubs them all over her beautiful, stunning, gorgeous face!

You won't find those instructions in this recipe but it's clear from my time with Rincy that it works.

This sambal that has so much freshness, depth and heritage within. It's on the menu every single day and I have fallen head over in love with how Rincy makes it.

She has the most beautiful energy when it comes to her traditional and food culture, and it's been a privilege to be taught this simple yet magnificent recipe . Nowadays whenever I pop over she already knows to ask when she sees me:

Chef – sambal and rice?

Yes, mate.

Hot chef?

Make it the way you were taught, mate.

Ooook chef!

Thank you Rincy for all the heat and laughter you have brought to my world.

Ingredients

1 lime, cut into pieces
1/2 cup fresh basil leaves
1-2 spring onions, sliced into
2 1/2cm pieces
1 small shallot, thinly sliced
2 cups cherry tomatoes,
quartered
2 red hot chilies
1 tbsp coconut oil
Salt and black pepper,
to taste
1 tbsp #EASE & FLOW

Method

Add all the ingredients to a bowl, mix well and serve.

PREP TIME 2-3mins
FREEZER-FRIENDLY No
R, RSF, NF

SERVES 1

Raw Miso Ginger Veggies

This dish is a beauty! You will feel like you're having authentic Asian takeaway – and that's the point. For the best experience, add the dressing just before you serve and mix it well with your hands (I dare you). If you like it spicy, add more cayenne.

The purpose of this recipe is for you to enjoy a flavourful meal, and most importantly, to experience the moment when your body says: Thank you for feeding my cells with real food ingredients!!

Ingredients

FOR THE VEGGIES:

10 green beans, sliced into bite-size pieces
1 carrot, sliced julienne
1/4 head of broccoli, cut into bite-size pieces
1 zucchini, sliced julienne
2 cups mung bean sprouts
1 chili, sliced, optional

FOR THE DRESSING:

1/4 cup unpasteurised shiro miso
1/4 cup olive oil
1/4 cup water
1 slice ginger
1 lime, juiced
2-3 tbsp maple syrup
1/4 cup almonds, soaked
1-2 tbsp tamari
A pinch of cayenne pepper
Salt and black pepper, to taste
1 tbsp #COMFORT

Method

TO PREPARE THE VEGGIES:

Add the ingredients to a bowl, season well and toss to combine. Set aside.

TO PREPARE THE DRESSING:

Add the ingredients to your blender and blend until combined, thick and creamy.

Drizzle over the veggies and serve.

PREP TIME 10-15 mins
FREEZER-FRIENDLY No
R, RSF, *NF
*NF – does not refer to the dressing

SERVES 1-2

Don't be afraid to use your hands when you're cooking. The true seasoning is in your hands.

Dips & "-isms"

Food connects us to people and places.
It brings friends and families together
over rituals and sharing to create
magnificent food memories.

Enjoy these Dips and fancy situations I've
created. They're even better when shared.

Quick Cucumber Pickle

I love pickles. They are a great addition to burger patties and salads and the liquid itself can be used for dressings as it's packed with flavour. When I think of store-bought pickles I immediately get the image of all sorts of flavour enhancers and other weird stuff. That's why I want you to embrace this recipe and start making your own pickles.

I used Bragg's organic raw unfiltered apple cider vinegar as I find that it's fantastic for this recipe. Give it a try!

Ingredients

1/2 cup apple cider vinegar

1 cucumber, thinly sliced

1/3 cup coconut sugar

1/4 cup fresh dill, roughly chopped

1 small shallot or 1/4 red onion, thinly sliced

Salt and black pepper, to taste

A pinch of #JOY

Method

Add the ingredients to a bowl and mix well.

Transfer to a jar or another container and make sure the liquid covers the cucumber.

Seal the container and store in the fridge for up to a week.

PREP TIME 5 mins
FREEZER-FRIENDLY No
R, RSF, NF

MAKES 400 ML

Mushroom Gravy

My mates love recipes like this. Their fast food days have come to an end but they still crave the simple things. This one's for my mate Rachelle. Give the woman mash potatoes with gravy and she will just about do anything for you.

I know the feeling. Enjoy!

Ingredients

1/4 cup raw cashews, soaked overnight and rinsed
1/4 onion, roughly diced
2 tbsp dried porcini powder*
1 small potato, peeled and chopped into bite-size chunks
1 tsp shiro miso paste
1 garlic clove, roughly chopped
1 tsp savoury yeast
2 cups water
Salt and black pepper, to taste
1 tbsp #ABUNDANCE
*Porcini is a mushroom that's been dried

Method

Add all the ingredients to a medium-size pot.

Cook on medium-high until the potato chunks are soft.

Turn off the heat and allow to rest for a few minutes.

Transfer to a blender and blend until completely smooth.

PREP TIME 5 mins
COOKING TIME 15-20 mins
FREEZER-FRIENDLY Yes
C, RSF

MAKES 600 ML

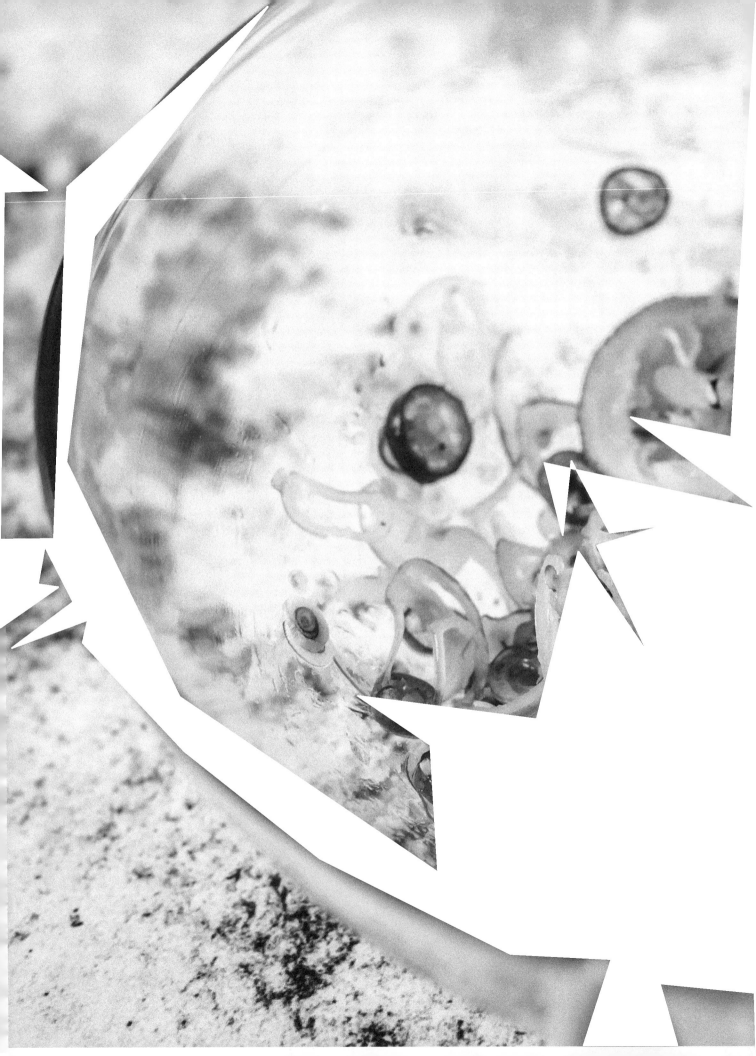

Sambal Matah

When I first tried sambal matah I nearly died. It was so hot in my mouth that it burnt all the way to my eyes and then along came a river of tears flowing down my face. I immediately ran for a jug of water to put out the fact that my whole face was on fire. That was nearly the end of a beautiful love story before it even began.

After living in Bali and hanging out with a bunch of home cooks and chefs, chilli slowly started finding its way in to my culinary world. Over time I absolutely fell in love with sambal matah. The brilliance of this little pocket of joy comes from just two elements. The first element is hot chilli. They give the recognisable fiery flavour with the aromatic scent of the lemongrass and kaffir lime leaves.

All that is rounded off with tangy shallots and refreshing lime that breaks the richness of coconut oil. It's epic!

The second key element is the seasoning in your hands. I know, right! Imagine all the ibus (mums) across Bali who use the same ingredients from the same village each time, but they make this dish with their hands and (more importantly) with intention, love and care for their families. This is what makes each version of sambal matah unique.

It's incredible! I couldn't believe it at first and spent days sitting on the floor eating this glory and trying to solve the puzzle – how come that it tastes differently even though the same ingredients are used?. This is when these kind and caring people, who are magnificent cooks by the way, taught me about the vibe of #intention.

Now I have different people make it in my studio and now I can recognise who made it based on the taste.

I want you to experience the joy of sambal matah but I have one tip: start with mild chilli like those long, fat ones. Then build your way up to those small, fiery chilies.

I'm already impatient to hear your stories!

Ingredients

1-2 shallots, thinly sliced

1 chili, sliced (the hotter your chili is, the better, at least for me)

1-2 tbsp coconut oil

1 kaffir lime leaf, thinly sliced

1 lemongrass stalk, thinly sliced

1 cheek of a lime

Salt, to taste

A pinch of #EASE & FLOW

Method

Add all the ingredients to a bowl and mix with your hands.

Massage and crush the ingredients while rubbing them with your fingers.

Serve with anything you like. I always go with rice and salad.

PREP TIME 5-7 mins
FREEZER-FRIENDLY No
R, RSF, NF

SERVES 1-2

Preserved Lemons

Here's the thing about preserved lemons: they're not the sort of thing you can just pick up anywhere. And while they're easy to make, it's not like you can just say, "Oh, I'll do them tomorrow afternoon and we'll have them on Thursday."

Way back in 2005 I worked in a health retreat, cooking, creating and learning from a bevy of talented and wise chefs and healers. One of those chefs was Yoland, a warm, welcoming woman in her 60s who was famous across the country.

She taught me how to preserve lemons. I thought it was a simple matter but my lemons would often grow moldy while hers remained perfect!

I know now that it's important to close the jar and leave them in a cool place for at least a month. Yoland would always say longer! The longer they are left, the better the flavor. And make sure they are covered! If a piece of lemon is not covered it develops a harmless white mold that needs to be washed off.

Make sure you use coarse salt, wash the lemons well, and allow them to dry before cutting and stuffing them with salt. If you don't succeed on your first attempt just keep going – preserved lemons are an essential item and they are so worth it.

Ingredients

1 clip lock jar, I used a 25cm one
8 lemons, quartered
Salt, 3 tbsp per lemon
6 lemons, juiced
A pinch of #INSPIRATION

Method

Quarter the lemons from the top to within 2cm of the bottom. Add salt to the exposed flesh, reshape the fruits and firmly push them into the jar.

Pour in the lemon juice and push the lemons down until they are covered with the juice.

Seal the jar and leave it on a shelf for 6 months. After 6 months, your preserved lemons are ready to be used.

PREP TIME 10 mins
FREEZER-FRIENDLY No
R, RSF, NF

MAKES 1 LITRE JAR

Chunky Dip

I frikking love this dip. Not only is it all things sweet, vinegary, and crunchy, it's also a fantastic dip to take to a party loaded with veggie sticks, corn chips, and crackers.

Some of my mates call it a next level spread for salad wraps. You be the judge.

Ingredients

FOR THE MAYO:

1/2 cup cashews,
soaked overnight,
rinsed and drained
1 tbsp dijon mustard
Water, as needed
Salt and black pepper,
to taste

FOR THE DIP:

1/2 cup sunflower seeds,
soaked overnight,
rinsed and drained
1/2 cup apple cider vinegar
1/4 cup maple syrup
1 small cucumber, diced
1 small celery stalk, diced
1/2 cup chopped fresh dill
leaves
1/4 red onion, finely diced
Salt and black pepper,
to taste
1 tbsp #FORGIVENESS

Method

TO PREPARE THE MAYO:

Add all the ingredients to the blender and blend until very smooth and creamy. Set aside.

TO PREPARE THE DIP:

Add the seeds to your food processor and pulse until a little chunky.

Transfer to a bowl and set aside.

Add the rest of the ingredients to the bowl together with the mayo, mix well and serve.

PREP TIME 5-8 mins
FREEZER-FRIENDLY No
R, RSF

SERVES 4

Spicy Tomato Chutney

Oh my sweet spicy chutney! This one will last in the fridge for weeks, and like the perfect handbag (or man-bag) you can take it everywhere.

I have brought this dish to BBQs, pot luck dinners, tapas platters, Indian dishes, on toast, in a salad bowl, and my absolute favourite: a platter with warm crusty sourdough a bowl of olive oil, seasoned with love, some dukka and a jar of this red glory. Heaven!

Ingredients

600g tomato, cut
into quarters
1/3 cup maple syrup
2 dates, torn into pieces
1-2 long, dried red chilies
1 garlic clove, smashed
A slice of ginger
2 tbsp apple cider vinegar
1/4 red chili, whole
1/4 green chili, whole
1 tbsp #LETTINGGO

Method

Add all the ingredients to a small pot and bring to the boil.

Turn down the heat to a simmer and cook for 12-15 minutes with the lid on.

When done, the chutney should have a jam-like consistency.

Allow to cool down, transfer to a jar and store in the fridge. It will last for 10 days.

PREP TIME 5 mins
COOKING TIME 10-15 mins
FREEZER-FRIENDLY No
C, RSF, NF

MAKES 1 CUP

Bean Dip

What makes this bean dip so special? I know it sounds crazy but it almost has a meaty flavour that mainly comes from the beans. You know how there are all sorts of veggie burgers out there made from beans and some of these recipes are actually pretty good and filling. So it looks like beans do the trick. Good job beans!

Although the recipe is super simple to make it's also very easy to mess up. Let's start with onions. They should be nicely browned or caramelised because you want the sweetness of onions to enrich the flavour of your bean dip. Onions need some time to release their sweetness but once they reach that point they can burn very quickly. Keep an eye on them and find that sweet spot where you get all the onion flavours booming.

The crucial thing for this dip to stay smooth is to keep it moist. The trick here is very simple: drizzle a generous amount of olive oil on top of your dip. It will prevent the dip from creating a crust on top.

If you do everything right the end result will be a dip with balanced flavours and freshness, with notes of parsley pulling through, just a hint of mustard sharpness, and a wonderful miso flavour. I'm pretty impressed with this recipe if I'm being totally honest! And I'm always honest .

Ingredients

2 tbsp olive oil
1 onion, finely chopped
3-4 garlic cloves, finely chopped
200g white beans, cooked and drained
200g red beans, cooked and drained
2-3 spring onions, finely chopped
1/2 cup fresh parsley, finely chopped
2 tbsp miso
1 tsp mustard
Salt and black pepper, to taste
A pinch of #PATIENCE

Method

Preheat a pan and add the olive oil along with the onion and garlic.

Season well with salt and pepper and cook until browned.

Stir in the beans, spring onions, parsley, and miso and cook for 3-5 more minutes.

Just before taking it off the heat, stir in the mustard and transfer the mixture to your food processor.

Blend until the ingredients are well combined and the dip has your desired texture.

Transfer to a container, drizzle with olive oil and top with some herbs if you wish.

Let cool down completely before keeping it in the fridge.

PREP TIME 5 mins
COOKING TIME 10-15 mins
FREEZER-FRIENDLY No
C, RSF, NF

SERVES 4

Bottom-of-the-fridge Pesto

*I was cleaning my veggie containers one day and found some lonely coriander and basil.
I use herbs to amp up my salads, wraps, and curries and now I was dealing with a bunch of
coriander and basil leftover down the bottom of the fridge.*

*My first thought was to throw them into the bin because they had lost their freshness.
On second thoughts, tossing out herbs that can still be used didn't seem right,
so I thought I'd create pesto.*

This was not my plan A but it sure was a damn great plan B.

I'll give you one tip here – if you feel the pesto is too thick add a tablespoon of water at a time.

Be careful because water makes fresh food go off fast, so adding more oil is also solution here.

*Use less oil and water to keep the pesto thick. It's damn good as a spread on wraps,
with corn chips or eggless omelette.*

The possibilities are almost endless. What are you doing with yours?

Ingredients

1/3 cup raw cashew nuts
A bunch of fresh coriander, roughly chopped
A handful of fresh basil leaves, roughly chopped
1 garlic clove
1 tsp savoury yeast
1/2 tsp maple syrup
1/2 lemon, juiced
2-3 tbsp olive oil
Water, as needed
Salt and black pepper, to taste
A pinch of #GRATEFULNESS

Method

Add all the ingredients to your food processor and pulse.

If the pesto seems to be too thick, add some water to reach the desired consistency.

Transfer to a jar and store in the fridge.

PREP TIME 5 mins
FREEZER-FRIENDLY No
R, RSF

MAKES 150-200ML

Black and White Gomasio

If you haven't tried gomasio before you are going to LOVE it. It's a simple, delightful moment of a flavour-packed seasoning that's so easy to make that it's ridiculous. You'll need only two ingredients – sesame seeds and salt, which marry together in the perfect balance of flavours. Like most things though, there is an art to making it. My friend, Chef Jelena, gave me some awesome tips that I'm passing onto you in this recipe. "Do not leave the stove and continue stirring on low heat and stay present." Then she would say: "Stop talking, Chef. You talk way too much, Chef".

YES, Chef Jelena.

Ingredients

1 tbsp salt
150g white sesame seeds
100g black sesame seeds
A pinch of #COMFORT

Method

Add the salt to a pan and cook on low heat for 5 minutes.

Add the sesame seeds and keep cooking and stirring.

Once the sesame seeds start changing colour, continue cooking and stirring for a few more minutes.

Turn off the heat half way though this cooking time and the residual heat will continue to cook the seeds.

Transfer to a tray and let cool for 5 minutes.

Transfer to a Suribachi (Japanese version of mortar and pestle), food processor or a mortar and pestle and grind the seeds into a powder, allowing a bit of texture.

Set aside to cool down. Store in a jar for months.

COOKING TIME 20 mins
FREEZER-FRIENDLY No
C, RSF, NF

SERVES MANY

Salt

I am an expert at using salt. I've ruined entire dishes by over-salting, under-salting, and even by using the wrong brand of salt in a favourite recipe.

You see not all salts were created equal.

I want to set you forth on an adventure to discover how you can create a masterpiece out of a simple dish by using the right kind of salt.

And while we're here you should know that adding your salt with a sprinkle of #goodintentions will transform your meals in to a glorious situation.

Let me introduce my good friend Daina, who spends most days sitting on my studio kitchen table (yes on it) watching me like a hawk.

As I cook or heat a dish she always pays attention, watches closely and observes what I am doing so she can create the same textures and flavours when she is cooking #smartwoman.

We've had many laughs together, eaten truly epic meals and will talk about human behaviour till the wee hours of the morning as we sip tea and eat homemade chocolates that have been seasoned with salt.

(My Next Level chocolate is made of pure cacao paste, cacao butter, a little sweetener and salt).

She is forever grateful for that life-changing lesson.

Daina is one friend that is always asking questions and commenting when I cook:

"Wow, how do you make that so tasty?"

"I made that recipe and it didn't turn out as good as yours"

Or

"Hey Cynth, what did you put in that dish?"

Before I can answer, our gazes will meet and in that moment she already has it "wait... waaaait... let me guess: Salt?!"

"Yes mate, it's salt".

She'll raise her hands in the air with a smirk on her face and in a loud voice declare "the secret salt that Chef Cynthia has".

I've taught thousands of people that salt is one of the building blocks of flavour, and more importantly, I've taught Daina how important it is to **mix her salts up.**

Practically it's like this: every time you run out of salt, don't buy the same brand again.

Experiment, explore, and discover for yourself. Here's just a short list of the incredible variety of salt that is available for us:

- pink Himalayan salt

- Maldon sea salt

- kosher salt

- fleur de sel

- grey salt

- Hawaiian black lava salt

- truffle salt

- smoked salt

Not to mention the salty flavours you'll find in

- soy sauce

- tamari

- shoyu

Salt carries with it the energy and flavours from its place of origin. Whether it's flakey crystals harvested from the sea, pink and black rocks from the Himalayas, or smokey salt imbued with local wood smoke, all the vast natural processes that have combined for its creation are captured in salt.

Chemically, salt is mainly sodium chloride, but your tongue will tell you there's an entire universe of difference between chemically refined table salt and crystals of lava salt from Hawaii or the large, flakey crystals of Maldon sea salt from the UK.

There's also a huge difference between cheap supermarket soy sauce and wheat-free organic Tamari from Spiral Foods.

So try it out for yourself and explore the world of salt.

And while you're at it, spare a thought for me as I'm writing this sitting on my couch in my undies and some random long sleeve shirt which I swear I didn't buy but just appeared in my closet.

I was going to google some facts on salt but you know what – apart from the fact that google makes me spin out, there's no way in hell googling something will tell you what it tastes like. Or how it combines with chocolate in the most epic way imaginable. Or which salt is perfect for you and your #goodintentions in every meal.

The best part is this – now that I've opened your eyes (just like Daina's), you're going to go on an adventure.

My friend Russ (a.k.a "The Great Writer Man" as he's known in my phone) is helping me write this book and he's already off to the shops hunting for smoky salt and Maldon salt flakes.

And that's what this is about. Less Google. More hunting for salty glories. More salt and #goodintentions in every meal.

You're the best.

Chef Cynthia Louise xx

There are 4 flavours:
Salty, sweet, sour and bitter ...
that's all you need to know.

Dinner

The human relationship with food is truly unique. The kitchen is not a stressful place but some of us make it so with our thoughts, feelings, and actions.

I've learnt to approach food with reverence. Gratitude for the farmers, gratitude for the wisdom of nature, gratitude for the many ways and traditions of cooking, gratitude for the way this food nourishes my body, my mind and my emotions, and gratitude for the friends and family I get to share all of this gratitude with!

When you come from this place of reverence, cooking and eating transforms your body, your heart, your relationships, your whole life.

Dinner has never tasted so good.

Yellow Rice

This is a traditional Indonesian dish we call nasi kuning. It's simple and easy – rice, lemongrass, garlic, turmeric and coconut milk – all melted together in a fusion of flavour and fragrance with a subtle exotic hint.

I use my rice cooker for preparing nasi kuning because it's easy and I don't have to be in the kitchen and keep an eye on it. If you don't have a rice cooker, worry not! You can still prepare this divine and velvety yellow rice by using the absorption cooking method. For those who are still newbies to cooking, this meansthat you bring the rice to the boil and then reduce the heat to very low, put the lid on and allow the rice to absorb all the moisture in the pot.

Whichever of these two cooking methods you choose, I'm sure you will enjoy this epic rice!

Ingredients

1 cup medium-grain rice, uncooked

1 lemongrass stalk

2 garlic cloves, smashed

3 tbsp turmeric juice*

2 cups coconut milk

2 tsp salt

1 tbsp #ABUNDANCE

*You can use 1 tsp Turmeric Powder instead

Method

Add all the ingredients to your rice cooker and stir to combine.

Press the Play button and cook following your cooker instructions.

When done, serve and EAT immediately!

PREP TIME 1 min

COOKING TIME Depends on your rice cooker

FREEZER-FRIENDLY No

C, RSF, NF

SERVES 2-3

Creamy Mushroom Pasta

How would I describe this mushroom pasta? It's creamy, packed with flavours, and filling. How do I feel when I eat this glory? That's a different story.

First, I can't tell there's no dairy in this recipe because what I taste resembles cream and cheese. What matters to me the most is that two servings later, I don't fall into that food coma. I bet that after eating something flavourful and savoury like pasta, you often say: Oh, I shouldn't have eaten so much. You won't feel that way after eating this epic mushroom pasta, and that's what makes the difference.

This is one of my most popular recipes and I regularly hear from my friends and fans writing in and sharing their stories of how they tricked their kids and partners into preferring this wholesome, dairy-free pasta to the traditional one. That feels like winning to me.

Ingredients

800ml water
1 cup cashews
Olive oil, for sautéing
1/2 big leek, thinly sliced
1/2 onion, sliced
5 garlic cloves, finely chopped
350g portobello mushrooms, thinly sliced
250g button mushrooms, thinly sliced
2 tbsp savoury yeast
Salt and black pepper, to taste
Gluten-free pasta of your choice
A pinch of #CARE

Method

Pour the water into your blender, add the cashews and blend until completely smooth and resembling milk. Set aside.

Heat a splash of olive oil in a pot on medium heat.

Add the leek, onions, and garlic, season with salt and pepper and sauté for 2 minutes.

Reduce the heat to medium-low, stir in the mushrooms and cook until the mushrooms release their natural liquid.

Pour in the cashew milk and cook on low simmer until the sauce thickens a bit.

Stir in the savoury yeast, taste and adjust the seasoning.

Flood your pasta with this magnificent sauce and enjoy this savoury treat!

PREP TIME 10-12 mins
COOKING TIME 15-20 mins
FREEZER-FRIENDLY Yes
C, RSF

SERVES 4

Lasagna

It took me some time to recreate this recipe, especially the bechamel sauce, but the outcome is magic. I have to say I was pretty amazed by the fact that you can use potatoes and cashews to create a creamy cheese sauce (by the way, the sauce is so good that you can use it in a cauliflower or veggie bake).

Now imagine this sauce in between lasagna sheets and a generous layer of meaty, mushroom sauce. It is irresistible, believe me.

This recipe has a special place in my heart because it reminds me of my dear friend and chef, Mel. A while ago we had a full day of filming for my online cooking classes, Mel was assisting, and the last recipe of the menu was this lasagna.

To this day, I vividly remember Mel saying:

Too hard, too much to prepare, Chef.

And then she continued with

I get home from work, I've got a kid to feed and then the last thing on the menu is lasagna, Chef.

You know, chefs are an odd bunch; we cook all day and the last thing we want to do when we come home is cook. So, this recipe is for you Mel and your daughter, little Stella. It's simple, it's swift, and it's full of #INSPIRATION.

I miss you Stella and Mel!

Ingredients

FOR THE CHEESE SAUCE:

1L water
1/4 onion, roughly chopped
1 garlic clove, crushed
300g potato, peeled and roughly chopped
1 cup raw cashew nuts
1/2 tsp nutmeg
1/4 cup savoury yeast
2 tsp salt
1/4 tsp black pepper

FOR THE NEAT SAUCE (AKA MEAT):

1 carrot, skin on
300g mushrooms
200g walnuts
Olive oil, for sautéing
1 large onion, roughly chopped
4 garlic cloves
1 tsp dried oregano
600ml tomato puree
1/4 cup Tomato Paste
1 tbsp balsamic vinegar
1 tbsp coconut sugar
Salt and black pepper, to taste
1 Tbsp #INSPIRATION

FOR THE ASSEMBLY:

250g gluten-free lasagna sheets, parboiled

Method

TO PREPARE THE CHEESE SAUCE:

Add the ingredients except the seasoning, nutmeg, and yeast to a pot and bring to the boil.

Turn down the heat to a simmer and cook until the potato is soft. Leave to rest and cool down.

Transfer to a blender, add the nutmeg and yeast and season with salt and pepper.

Blend until well combined and smooth and set aside.

TO PREPARE THE NEAT SAUCE:

Add one mushroom and carrot at a time to your food processor, pulse until the texture resembles breadcrumbs, and transfer to a bowl.

Add the walnuts to the food processor, pulse until they turn into crumbs and transfer to the bowl with veggies.

Pour olive oil in a pan and heat on medium.

Add the onion and garlic and sauté until translucent.

Stir in the processed carrot, mushrooms, and walnuts.

Add the oregano and continue to stir and cook for around 3-5 minutes.

Pour in the tomato puree and paste and mix well.

Add the balsamic vinegar and coconut sugar and season with salt, pepper, and more oregano if you wish.

Sauté for a few more minutes until all the ingredients are cooked through. Set aside.

TO ASSEMBLE:

Preheat the oven at 170C / 340F.

Lay parboiled lasagna sheets on the bottom of a baking dish (size 25 x 5 x 5 cm).

Spread 1/3 of the cheese sauce on top followed by the neat sauce.

Repeat with the laying process and end with the cheese sauce.

Bake in the preheated oven for 1 hour.

Allow to rest for 10 minutes before serving.

PREP TIME 15 mins
COOKING TIME 1 hour
FREEZER-FRIENDLY Yes
C, RSF

SERVES 4-6

Tofu Larb

This dish is the one that I pull together fast. The longer I cook it, the more the tofu goes dry. In this case that's a good thing as it will absorb more flavour.

Savour the spicy and sweet notes as well as the wonderfully full flavour that coriander brings to this dish.

And to cap it all, a super important part that it brings it all home is the freshly squeezed lime.

My team can't get enough of this recipe and request it often. I love to make it, and so will you.

Ingredients

Coconut or olive oil,
for sautéing
1 packet firm tofu, crumbled
1/4 cup coconut sugar
1-2 tbsp apple cider vinegar
2-3 tbsp tamari
2 large red shallots,
finely chopped
4 garlic cloves, grated
2 1/2cm ginger, grated
A bunch of fresh coriander,
roughly chopped
Freshly squeezed lime juice,
as much as you like
1 lime, quartered,
for serving
1 chili, sliced, for serving
Wong bok, for serving
A pinch of #JOY

Method

Heat the oil in a pan, add the tofu and cook for 5-8 minutes.

Stir in the coconut sugar, pour in the apple cider vinegar and cook for 2 more minutes.

Pour in the tamari, give it a stir and then add the shallots, garlic, and ginger and sauté for 5 more minutes.

Turn off the heat, add the coriander and drizzle in the lime juice.

Serve your larb in wong bok leaves with some chili slices and lime wedges.

PREP TIME 2-3 mins
COOKING TIME 15 mins
FREEZER-FRIENDLY No
C, RSF, NF

SERVES 2

Spag Bowl

A classic Aussie dish that's served at least once a week to nearly every kid I have ever met. Ask any grown-up from Australia and I bet they'll remember their mum's spag bowl recipe.

Many a mum has tried to smuggle in extra peas and carrots to get more veggies into their kids. This recipe is inspired by a landmark restaurant in Ubud – the foodies Mecca of Bali. They've been making elegant plant-based meals at The Elephant for years and they keep doing it right.

I sat down at a table surrounded by hippies playing with their crystals and people from the 9-5 who came for a week and stayed for a year.

On the menu was spaghetti bolognese and it was so delicious I had to recreate it at home.

Now it's about to arrive in your home.

Ingredients

2 tbsp olive oil
200g onion, finely chopped
20g garlic, finely diced
1 1/2 tbsp dried oregano
350g carrots, finely chopped
1 head cauliflower, processed into crumbs
200g button mushrooms, processed into crumbs
1 celery stick, finely diced
600ml tomato puree
2 tbsp balsamic vinegar
2-3 tsp maple syrup
3-4 tbsp tomato paste
1 cup fresh basil leaves
1 packet GF spaghetti, boiled according to packet instructions*
Olive oil, for serving
1 cup #FAITH
*You can use kelp or rice noodles or any noodles of choice

Method

Heat the oil in a large pan on medium-high.

Add the onions, garlic, and oregano, stir well and sauté for a couple of minutes.

Add the rest of your veggies, season well and cook for 5-8 minutes.

Stir in the remaining ingredients except the basil, taste again and cook for 15 minutes stirring occasionally.

Cook your pasta, strain and toss with a little olive oil, chopped basil, salt, and pepper.

Flood the pasta with your veggie sauce and serve immediately.

PREP TIME 5 mins
COOKING TIME 30 mins
FREEZER-FRIENDLY Yes
C, RSF, NF

SERVES 4-6

Eat food you recognise.

Roasted Trees & Bulbs

Trees and Bulbs aka roasted broccoli and cauliflower with whole, skin-on garlic cloves. Let's talk about why this simple recipe has a special place in my kitchen. My days sometimes keep going and going and suddenly I feel hungry and tired at the same time. Cooking feels like a painful experience in such moments.

Luckily, I have developed some default recipes over time that swiftly take me to a place of #ABUNDANCE. This is one of such recipes – one tray and an oven are the key to this simple, achievable, excellent-in-flavour dish that is genius when one is tired.

Now, the name... I knew you were curious. Let's talk about the title of the recipe, shall we?

My friends are an interesting bunch. Some of them are crap cooks that don't have time to prepare their own meals, so they have cooks that prepare my recipes for them! My other friends cook but honestly, they have no idea what they are doing. When they are in the kitchen, they are a danger to themselves and others; they forget small, important things like the names of ingredients.

My friend Daina, however, is one of those humans who names ingredients in codes. She is ex-Navy, so this habit of hers kind of makes sense.

Now we come to the part of the story where you learn how the name of this recipe came about.

Daina's messages on Whatsup: I will bring the green trees. What's those small yellow things called again? Chef?

I stare at my phone while she continues typing.

Daina: Cause I see the brown ones, green ones, white ones, but there are no yellow ones. Chef? Chef?

Me: What the hell are you talking about woman?!

I'm glad I invested in our friendship as her "code" words make me laugh so much that my belly hurts (in a good way). She brings such a great vibe to my cooking world that her wacky words end up becoming titles of my published recipes.

This one's for you, Daina!

Ingredients

1/2 head of broccoli
cut into florets
1/2 head of cauliflower
cut into florets
1 knob of garlic, whole
unpeeled (around 10 cloves)
olive oil
salt and pepper

Method

Preheat your oven to 350F/180C.

Line a large tray with baking paper and set aside.

Add all the ingredients to a bowl and toss to coat
the veggies with the oil.

Transfer to the baking tray and bake for 45-50 minutes
or until golden and cooked through.

PREP TIME 5 mins
COOKING TIME 45-50 mins
FREEZER-FRIENDLY No
R, RSF, NF

SERVES 4

Rendang

A classic Indonesian dish – smooth, coconutty and fragrant, this will bring the warm scent of the tropics in to the coldest of hearts and the hungriest of mouths.

Ingredients

FOR THE PASTE:

4-6 garlic cloves, whole
10g ginger, sliced
15g galangal ginger, sliced
1/4 red onion or 6 red shallots, roughly chopped
1 long red chili, seeds removed, roughly chopped
2 lemongrass stalks, use only the bottom part, roughly chopped
5 dried chilies, seeds removed, soaked in 1/4 cup water for 8-10 minutes (don't discard the water)

FOR THE CURRY:

1 cup desiccated coconut
1/4 cup coconut oil, for frying the paste
4 kaffir lime leaves, crushed
1 packet tempeh, cut into large cubes
200g mushrooms, quartered
3 tbsp maple syrup
3 tbsp tamari
1 tbsp curry powder
800ml coconut milk
Salt and black pepper, to taste
1 tsp #JOY

Method

TO PREPARE THE PASTE:

Add all the ingredients (together with the water in which you soaked the chilies) to your blended and blend until well combined.

Set aside until ready to be used.

TO PREPARE THE CURRY:

Toast the desiccated coconut for a couple of minutes or until golden brown.

Transfer to your blender, pulse a couple of times and set aside.

Heat a large pot on low-medium and add the coconut oil.

Pour the paste into the pot (at this point the paste should swim in the oil). Cook for 5-6 minutes and stir continuously.

Add the curry leaves, tempeh, mushrooms, toasted coconut, maple syrup, tamari, curry powder, and coconut milk.

Stir well to combine everything, taste and season with salt and pepper if needed.

Turn down the heat to a low simmer and cook for 45-60 minutes. Stir occasionally to prevent burning.

When done, serve over a bed of rice or quinoa.

PREP TIME 10 mins
COOKING TIME 1 hour
FREEZER-FRIENDLY No
C, RSF, NF

SERVES 2-4

Potato Bake

I created this potato bake with my friend Courtney in an epic moment of genius!
It was actually Courtney's mum, Heather, who inspired us to give this recipe a try.
Courtney always talks about her mum's famous potato bake and I just felt
so tempted to try this recipe.

I'll just say this – when it was ready we could barely let it cool down, so we ate
immediately and even though it was burning our mouths we scoffed every single bite.
The real star of the dish is the cashew cream. It's wonderful how savoury this
dish gets thanks to a simple mixture of cashews and water.

There is one trick that I learnt from Heather. She taught me to push
the veggies down so that they are covered in juice. The magic happens
when the veggies soak up all these wonderful flavours.

Go and give this recipe a try – I think you'll love it as much as I do.

Ingredients

2 cups cashews
750ml water
2 tbsp savoury yeast
850g small potatoes, unpeeled, cut into thin slices
15 large mushrooms, thinly sliced
1 onion, thinly sliced
3-5 garlic cloves, roughly chopped
1 red capsicum, sliced julienne
1 red chilli, deseeded, finely diced
1/2 tsp salt
1/2 tsp black pepper
1 tbsp sweet paprika
1 tbsp #GRATITUDE

Method

Preheat your oven to 170C/340F. Have a baking tray ready to go (I used the size 35 x 25 x 10 cm).

Add the cashews, water, and savoury yeast to a blender, blend until completely smooth and creamy and set aside.

Combine the veggies into a large bowl, flood them with the cashew cream and toss to coat.

Season with salt and pepper, transfer to your tray and sprinkle with the paprika and more savoury yeast if you wish.

Cover with foil and bake for 45-60 minutes or until the veggies are fork-tender.

When done, leave to rest for 8-10 minutes.

Gather your family, serve and enjoy this glory.

PREP TIME 10-15 mins
COOKING TIME 45-60 mins
FREEZER-FRIENDLY No
C, RSF

SERVES 4-6

Not Butter Chicken

Reuben is my camera guy (I call him my Cameraman Of Glory)
– born and raised in Bombay, India. Over the years we've
worked together Reuben regularly speaks of his mum's cooking.
He tells me stories of his childhood meals and the hustle of downtown
Bombay with streets filled with chai wallahs pouring glasses
of chai from impossible heights.

I remember a fleeting moment filming on set in the studio.
No words shared just a quick glance that translated to

Reuben – let's see how you pull this off Chef!

Chef – challenge accepted Reuben

When he tasted it he looked at me and said

This is good. Really good. It's just missing one thing. Chicken.

I love you, Reuben, I treasure how much you have added to my career,
how your ideas keep rolling in and how at times we disagree on things.

You have been there by my side at times in my darkest hours,
seen me at my worst on set and captured my best. You have introduced
me to your family and invited me over to have time with your mum
in the kitchen. You are one of the sweetest humans I know.

Thank you for your palette and our disagreements
on who makes the best chai. This one's for you.

Ingredients

1 cup raw cashews

500ml water

2 tomatoes, roughly chopped

1 red chili, roughly chopped, optional

1/3 cup organic tomato paste

Coconut oil, for frying

1 onion, thinly sliced

4 garlic cloves, finely chopped

2 tbsp sweet paprika

1 cinnamon stick

1/2 tsp cinnamon powder

1 tsp fennel seeds

6 whole cardamom pods, crushed

1/2 tsp cayenne pepper

2 tbsp maple syrup

2 tbsp coriander powder

Salt and black pepper, to taste

3 large carrots, cut into bite-size chunks, steamed

3 large potatoes, cut into bite-size chunks, steamed

1 tbsp #GRATITUDE

PREP TIME 8 mins
COOKING TIME 50-60 mins
FREEZER-FRIENDLY Yes
C, RSF

Method

Add the cashews, water, tomatoes, chili, and tomato paste to your blender.

Blend until completely smooth and creamy. Set aside.

Heat a medium-sized pan over high heat and pour in some coconut oil.

Add the onions, garlic, and spices and season with salt and pepper.

Cook over medium heat for 5 minutes stirring continuously to avoid burning.

Reduce the heat to low and cook for 5 more minutes.

Stir in the creamy cashew sauce and cook for 20 minutes stirring constantly.

Add your steamed veggies and allow to cook for 30 more minutes over low heat. Keep stirring to prevent the sauce from sticking to the bottom.

When the cooking time is up, turn off the heat and allow to rest before serving.

Serve with beautifully steamed rice or quinoa.

MAKES 1L OF SAUCE

Detox Lentil Soup

Whenever something has detox in its name I immediately think it's something with zero flavour.

Well, it may be true for some things out there, but let me tell you there's NO place for anything with zero flavour within a hundred miles of this cookbook OK!

This lentil soup will make your taste buds sing with joy. How do we create flavours? In this soup, you will use that time tested combination of onions, garlic, celery, and fresh parsley. It's like nature's stock. Combined with salt and pepper – our building blocks of flavour – and you won't need anything else.

I teach these type of skills during my online cooking classes and it's always such a heart-warming feeling to see people's eyes sparkle with joy of this new discovery.

So, you see, you can have a detox soup and still enjoy a flavoursome meal. It's so filling and nourishing you won't crave anything else.

Ingredients

Olive oil, for cooking

1 onion, diced

4 garlic cloves, finely chopped

1/2 cup brown lentils, soaked overnight

1.5L water

2 medium carrots, finely chopped

1 stalk celery, finely chopped

1 large zucchini, finely chopped

2 tomatoes, roughly chopped

Salt and black pepper, to taste

1/2 bunch of fresh flat-leaf parsley, roughly chopped, for garnishing

1 cup #CONTENTMENT

Method

Preheat a pot on medium-high and drizzle in some oil.

Add the onions and garlic and cook until translucent.

Season with salt and pepper and continue cooking for one more minute.

Add the lentils and water, taste and season with more salt if needed.

Bring to the boil, reduce to a simmer and cook with a lid on for 45-60 minutes.

When the lentils are cooked through, add the carrot and celery cook for 10 more minutes.

Stir in the zucchini and tomatoes and cook on high heat for 5 more minutes.

Add the parsley, stir, and EAT!

PREP TIME 5 mins

COOKING TIME 50-60 mins

FREEZER-FRIENDLY Yes

C, NF, RSF

SERVES 5

I love Rice, I can't live without it.

Mexican Rice

The story of this recipe starts years ago at one health retreat where people were water fasting. There was one lady who was on her 21st day of fast, so her energy was diminished as you might expect. I talked to her and found out she is passionate about food and cooking. I took her to my kitchen and a strange and beautiful thing happened – she perked up, her senses woke up and all her love for food came out. On that day, she taught me how to make Mexican rice.

If you ask me about the key ingredient that makes this rice so irresistibly delicious, I won't have the answer to that. The ingredients fuse together perfectly and each of them plays an equally important role.

One thing I do know is how much this dish has nourished my organs and mind. I will never forget the stories of how this woman fasted on water for 21 days and shared all her food stories and culture with me as she cooked this dish. It's epic and made of glorious wholefood ingredients, just the way we love it.

Ingredients

FOR THE SAUCE:

2 long red chilies, whole
2 hot chilies, whole
1 red capsicum, chopped
into large pieces
2 tomatoes, cut into
quarters
5 garlic cloves, smashed*

FOR THE RICE:

Olive oil, for sautéing**
2 onions, finely chopped
1 cup long-grain rice
1 tsp cumin powder
1 tsp coriander powder
1 tsp smoked paprika
1 1/2 cups water
Salt and black pepper,
to taste
A bunch of fresh coriander,
for garnishing
A pinch of #FORGIVENESS

*You can use more for a
stronger flavour
**More oil may be needed
for frying the onions and
rice

Method

TO PREPARE THE SAUCE:

Preheat your oven at 180C/350F.

Line a baking tray with unbleached baking paper.

Place the chilies, capsicum, tomatoes, and garlic into the tray
and bake for 25 minutes.

Transfer to a blender, blend until smooth and set aside.

TO PREPARE THE RICE:

Preheat a pan on medium-high, pour in the oil and add the
onions, rice and season well. Stir-fry until browned.

Add the cumin, coriander and paprika and stir-fry for one
more minute.

Transfer all the ingredients together with the sauce to a rice
cooker, pour in the water, taste and adjust the seasoning.

Give it a stir, press the Play button and cook following you
rice cooker instructions.

Serve garnished with coriander and EAT!

PREP TIME 1 min
COOKING TIME 15 mins (depends
on your rice cooker)
BAKING TIME 25 mins
FREEZER-FRIENDLY No
C, RSF, NF

SERVES 2

White Soup

I learned how to make this soup years ago in a heath retreat where I used to work. We usually made it with Brazil nuts and the flavour was epic. At the time I was making the soup on my own I had only cashews and it still turned out to be magnificent.

The nuts are the key in this soup because they create a charming, creamy flavour and the texture is just sublime. A big tip I can give you is to let the soup rest for 10 minutes to allow the flavours to mingle before you blend.

Remember that soup needs to be creamy, so you'll need to blend it for a bit longer to get rid of the texture from the nuts.

I once served this white soup in shot glasses with a couple of drops of olive oil and a sprinkle of spring onion slices. Everyone licked the glasses and asked for more. That's how good this soup is!

Ingredients

Coconut oil, for sautéing
1 onion, roughly chopped
5 garlic cloves, minced
1 large or 2 small heads of cauliflower, roughly chopped
1 1/2 cups raw cashews
Salt and black pepper, to taste
1 tbsp #PATIENCE

Method

Heat the coconut oil on medium heat.

Add the onion and garlic, season with salt and pepper, and cook for 3 minutes. Stir continuously and make sure that the onions don't burn.

Add the chopped cauliflower, mix well and cook for a minute before adding cashews.

Pour in enough water to cover the veggies, stir well, taste and add more salt if needed.

Bring to the boil and cook for 5 minutes. Lower the heat to a simmer and cook for 5-8 more minutes.

When ready, leave the soup to rest for 10 minutes.

Transfer to a food processor and blend until completely smooth and creamy.

Treat your body with a bowl of this glorious soup.

PREP TIME 5-8 mins
COOKING TIME 10 mins
FREEZER-FRIENDLY Yes
C, RSF

SERVES 4

Peas & Rice

I grew up on rice, not potatoes and bread.
To this day I'm a loyal lover of this tiny yet magnificent grain.
In Bali, where I live now, the main component of almost any meal is rice.

It's such a simple yet versatile ingredient that allows you to unleash your
creativity in the kitchen. My rice and peas meal calls for only a couple of
ingredients but let me tell you; this is such an epic tapestry of flavour.

Whenever I make it, it barely makes it out of the pan because it gets
scoffed so quickly. When I'm not eating it straight out of the pan
I'll serve it with my pineapple curry or coconut lentil stew.

Now, let's have a couple of words on tempering, which is widely used in
Indian cuisine. It's a method of cooking whole or ground spices in hot oil
and pouring them over a finished dish for extra flavour. The only thing you
need to keep in mind here is not to burn the spices because they will go bitter.
If you do, you'll need to throw them away and start over.

So, to get this step right, you need to know your stove really well
and be present in the NOW. Treat tempering like a little meditation.
Pay close attention to your breath, the hot oil, the spices, the aromas,
the heat – to everything that is unfolding in this wonderful existence of ours
– and you'll create the most perfect flavour anywhere – the flavour of NOW.

Ingredients

Coconut oil, for frying
1 1/2 cups rice, cooked
2 cups peas, blanched
1 tsp cumin powder
Salt and black pepper,
to taste
1/2 tsp nigella seeds
1/2 tsp mustard seeds
Curry leaves
1 tbsp #EASE & FLOW

Method

Add a splash of oil to a pan and heat on medium.

Add the rice, peas, and cumin powder, season with salt and pepper and cook for a couple of minutes until the flavours combine. Set aside.

In a separate pan, heat a splash of oil on medium-high, add the seeds and curry leaves and fry until fragrant.

Drizzle over your rice and peas and EAT!

PREP TIME 10-15 mins
COOKING TIME 5 mins
FREEZER-FRIENDLY No
C, RSF, NF

SERVES 2

Yellow Curry

*The colour of the sun and the scent of heaven
(if heaven had a scent it would smell like this curry)...*

*I was taught this recipe years ago by all the Ibu's I have ever sat with
on a hard kitchen floor surrounded by nothing but earth, a chopping board,
a mortar and a pestle. An Ibu is a mother or a female elder in Indonesia.
In Bali the traditional name is Memek.*

*We would grind down a spice mix called bumbu genap Bali, which means
complete seasoning, and those moments are some of the greatest food experiences
of my life. It was such an honour to be on the family compound floor with so many
women creating a vibe of joy and care when it comes to cooking.*

*Just about everything you can imagine is used in this mix. It forms a marinade
for flavouring pigs (none in this recipe book), chicken, goat, fish, tempeh, tofu,
veggies, rice and everything savoury you conceive.*

*An almost sacred spice blend that is passed down from Memek to Memek,
bumbu genap Bali is the most used and created mix in Bali. Its scent will have
you walking in a trance till you find the source of its maker.*

It's incredibly beautiful with such rich flavour and culture.

*Food culture brings to my world a deep feeling of respect and gratitude.
Growing up in Papua New Guinea and now living in Bali, I am surrounded
by villages full of incredible home cooks that all have their secret ways of
making dishes that are generations old.*

*This is my version of Yellow Curry. There is no way I could make this dish in the
traditional way (we'd have to be sitting on the floor for starters) – but I have served
it all through Bali to many a Memek and they all gave it their seal of approval.*

Enjoy this precious meal with respect and care to all.

PREP TIME 10 mins
COOKING TIME 15-20 mins
FREEZER-FRIENDLY Yes*
*Paste is, but curry is not
C, RSF, NF

MAKES: 150ML OF PASTE
SERVES 2 - 4

Ingredients

FOR THE PASTE:

2 1/2cm fresh galangal
ginger root, peeled and
roughly chopped

5cm fresh turmeric root,
peeled and roughly chopped

5cm fresh ginger root,
chopped

60g shallots, roughly
chopped

4 garlic cloves, peeled

4-5 long red chilies, chopped
roughly (optional)

2 small red hot chilies,
chopped roughly (optional)

1 lemongrass stalk, bottom
part, roughly chopped

1 tbsp coriander seeds

1 tsp coriander powder

Water, as needed

1/4 cup coconut oil

3 kaffir lime leaves

FOR THE CURRY:

1 potato, chopped into
bite-size chunks

1/2 carrot, chopped into
bite-size chunks

750ml coconut milk

1 block tempeh, chopped
into bite-size chunks

1 lemongrass stalk, upper
part, smashed and tied
into a knot

1 tbsp maple syrup

1 cup water

1/4 zucchini, chopped into
bite-sized pieces

1/2 red capsicum, cut into
cubes

6 button mushrooms, halved

Salt and black pepper,
to taste

FOR GARNISHING:

Fresh coriander leaves
Fresh red chilies
A pinch of #POSITIVITY

Method

TO PREPARE THE PASTE:

Add the ingredients in a blender and blend until smooth. Pour in a bit of water if needed to bring the ingredients together.

Add the coconut oil and the paste to a pot and turn the heat to low.

Add the kaffir lime leaves and cook for 10 minutes while stirring continuously.

Keep 1/4 cup of the paste in the pot and use it for preparing your curry. Store the rest in the fridge or freezer for future use.

TO PREPARE THE CURRY:

Add the potatoes and carrots to the paste.

Pour in half of the coconut milk, add the tempeh and bring to a boil.

Turn down the heat to a simmer, pour in the rest of the coconut milk and cook for a couple of minutes.

Add the lemongrass and maple syrup and cook until the potatoes are just soft.

Pour in the water, add the remaining ingredients, taste and adjust the seasoning if needed.

Let the curry simmer until the potatoes are really soft.

Garnish, serve immediately and enjoy this epic curry.

Green Goddess Soup

This is my go-to soup – vibrant and swamp-like in colour, served with a splash of coconut yogurt and fresh herbs. I especially love the fact that I can make it in advance, freeze it and have it anytime I feel like my organs needs a warm and nourishing hug.

Besides being a fulfilling dinner this soup makes a great snack. You're probably thinking how a soup can be a snack. Well, this one can. If you're thinking about shedding some weight, have this soup regularly and you won't feel like you are on some sort of a diet. It's very nourishing and that's what should matter.

Our bodies start changing when we start giving them the nourishment they need. If you have this soup in the early afternoon, as a snack before the dinner, it will get you more alkaline so you won't crave sh*tty fast food.

Soon enough, your body will start changing and glowing. Your energy will lift, your weight will drop. This is your body's way of saying thank you for nourishing it with great food.

Ingredients

2l water
1 head of broccoli, stalk included, chopped into big chunks
1 large zucchini, chopped into big chunks
1 small leek, both green and white parts, thinly sliced
1 cup frozen peas
2 garlic cloves, smashed
A handful of button mushrooms
A big bunch of baby spinach
1 cup #ACCEPTANCE

Method

Pour the water into a pot and bring it to the boil.

Add all the veggies except the spinach and cook for about 4 minutes or until the broccoli is just soft.

Turn off the heat, add the spinach, stir and let it sit for 5 minutes.

Drain, keep the cooking water and transfer the veggies to the blender.

Blend until smooth, pouring in as much cooking water as needed to reach your desired consistency.

Serve this hug in a bowl immediately and enjoy!

PREP TIME 2-3 mins
COOKING TIME 5-8 mins
FREEZER-FRIENDLY Yes
C, RSF, NF

SERVES 4

Mushroom Bourguignon

*I'm not sure why this French dish spiked my interest one day as I was pottering
in my kitchen studio. It might have been the kilograms of porcini mushrooms
my mate Chef Mel brought for me, sitting on my shelf and staring at me.
Whatever the reason was, I'm glad I gave this classic dish a crack.*

*To be clear, there's nothing traditional about my version of bourguignon. However, my
French friends say it reminds them of their grandmother's cooking, and that's enough for
me to pass this recipe onto you. It has a slightly bitter edge because of the wine and porcini
powder, but it's an excellent dish for colder months as it cuddles you from inside out.*

*By the way, mushroom bourguignon and mash potato are a match made in heaven.
Here's a quick tip – you'll make a super creamy mash by using a ricer (google it),
adding a bit of coconut cream, a splash of olive oil, a few slices of spring onions,
salt and pepper and #LOVE. You are good to go!*

Ingredients

Olive oil, for sautéing
3 large or 10 small red
shallots, thinly sliced
8 garlic cloves, grated
2 carrots, sliced
6 sprigs of fresh thyme
400g button mushrooms,
sliced
3 tbsp tomato puree
2 tbsp rice flour
3 tbsp porcini powder
2 cups red wine
500ml water
Salt and black pepper,
to taste
1 tbsp coconut sugar
or maple syrup
1 cup #COMFORT

Method

Heat a pot on medium and add a splash of olive oil.

Add the shallots, garlic, carrots, and thyme and cook for
5 minutes. Stir continuously to avoid browning.

Add the mushrooms and sauté for 10-15 more minutes.

Season with salt and pepper, stir in the tomato puree, flour,
and porcini powder and cook for 1 more minute.

Turn up the heat, pour in the wine and stir well to combine.

Pour in the water, taste and adjust with sweetener and
seasonings.

Turn down the heat to low and cook for 15 minutes with
the lid on.

Serve warm.

PREP TIME 5 mins
COOKING TIME 45-60 mins
FREEZER-FRIENDLY No
C, RSF, NF

SERVES 2

Coconut Lentil Soup

There is an art to food photography which no one talks about and that is eating the captured dish. I found myself at the end of this particular day scoffing mouthfuls of this rich, hearty, budget-friendly soup before anyone else had a chance to dive in. It's that good!

I recommend adding just a bit of spice to bring out the richness of the coconut milk. I also add extra curry powder just because I like it.

Trust me, this is comfort food at its finest.

Ingredients

Coconut oil, for sautéing
1 onion, finely diced
2 garlic cloves, grated
2 1/2cm piece ginger, grated
3 cups water
500ml coconut milk
1/2 cup brown lentils, soaked in 200ml water for at least 2 hours or overnight
1/2 cup red split peas
3 tsp curry powder
1 tsp cumin powder
1/4 tsp cayenne pepper
200g baby spinach
1/2 lemon, juiced
A bunch of fresh coriander, chopped, for garnish
Salt and black pepper, to taste
1 tbsp #PEACE

Method

Preheat a small pot on medium and add a splash of coconut oil.

Add the onion, garlic, and ginger and season well.

Sauté until the onion has become translucent.

Pour in the water and coconut milk, add the lentils and split peas, mix in the spices and simmer with the lid on for 35 minutes.

Fold in the spinach and coriander, drizzle in the lemon juice and serve.

PREP TIME 8 mins
COOKING TIME 40 mins
FREEZER-FRIENDLY Yes
C, RSF, NF

SERVES 4

Cauliflower Rice

I don't google food trends and fads. I don't follow the latest hippy food bloggers and I'm definitely allergic to green goddess active-wearing smoothie-peddling insta-celebrities too.

Just give me real food the way nature intended and I'll turn it into delicious situations without all the fuss.

When it came to cauliflower rice I was blissfully unaware that it was on hipster menus from Bondi to Bali.

I'd just made my Pineapple Curry and Donna happened to be on set as we were filming my online class "Let's EAT Light & Easy". I was looking for something to go with it besides rice or quinoa, so she pipes up:

Cauliflower rice – make that.

Make what?!

Donna explained. I listened. And the rest is history.

Ingredients

1 head of cauliflower, chopped into chunks
1 cup #INSPIRATION

Method

Using the grated blade, grate the cauliflower in your food processor.

Fill a pot with water, bring it to the boil and add the cauliflower rice.

Boil for 5 minutes, strain and discard the water.

Serve with a generous amount of your favourite curry.

PREP TIME 2 mins
COOKING TIME 5 mins
FREEZER-FRIENDLY No
C, RSF, NF

SERVES 2

If it's real food, eat it.

Pineapple Curry

*This unforgettable dish is sweet, spicy, savoury and heavenly all at once.
The pineapple stays super juicy and bursts in your mouth.
It's refreshing and won't make you feel heavy.*

*The hardest part of this is the tempering (that and keeping the
curry fans the hell away from eating it all).*

*The first time I tempered anything I burnt the hell out of all the spices.
So just start again if that's you – you'll pick it up in no time.*

*I will confess I like this dish even more the day after.
That's the magic thing about curries – they taste even better
as left overs. Just whip it up with my fantastic cauliflower rice
and you've got a dead set winner every time.*

*A final word about curry leaves. They are incredible.
My advice is to hunt down a plant and plant as many as you can
in the garden. You will have these babies on tap for ever!*

*If you can't find a curry plant and only see the leaves sold in shops, you can
freeze them in a plastic bag and pull them out for the next curry night.*

Ingredients

FOR THE SPICE PASTE:

1 cup desiccated coconut
1 medium onion, roughly chopped
1 green chili, roughly chopped, you can add more if you like spicy
3cm slice ginger root
1 garlic clove
3 tbsp water

FOR THE CURRY:

1/2 ripe pineapple, cut into bite-size pieces
1/4 cup coconut sugar
1/4 cup water
1/2 tsp chili powder
1/2 tsp turmeric powder
1/2 tsp cumin powder
2 cups coconut milk
Salt and black pepper, to taste

FOR THE TEMPERING:

1 tbsp coconut oil
1-2 shallots, finely sliced
2-3 dried chilies, optional
1/2 tsp mustard seeds
1/4 tsp fenugreek seeds
1 sprig of fresh curry leaves
1 tbsp #COURAGE

Method

TO PREPARE THE SPICE PASTE:

Add the ingredients to a food processor or blender and blend until a paste is formed.

Transfer to a small bowl and set aside.

TO PREPARE THE CURRY:

Add the pineapple, coconut sugar, water, and chili, turmeric, and cumin powders to a medium-size pan.

Season with salt and pepper and cook on low heat for about 15 minutes or until the pineapple is infused with spices.

Stir in the spice paste and cook for another 8-10 minutes.

Pour in the coconut milk, stir well, and continue cooking on low for 5 more minutes.

*The cooking time for the curry may vary by 5-10 minutes depending on how ripe your pineapple is. If your pineapple is very ripe, reduce the cooking time. If the pineapple is less ripe, increase the cooking time.

TO PREPARE THE TEMPERING:

In a separate pot, heat the oil on low heat, add the shallots, dried chilies, mustard and fenugreek seeds, and fry for 2 minutes or until the shallots turn golden brown. Make sure not to burn the spices, as they will go bitter.

Add the curry leaves and fry for a few seconds, stirring continuously to prevent burning.

Immediately pour over the pineapple curry, stir to combine and serve with the cauliflower rice.

PREP TIME 5-10 mins
COOKING TIME 25-30 mins
FREEZER-FRIENDLY No
C, RSF, NF

SERVES 3-4

Pea & Coconut Soup

Pea lovers will fall in love with this soup. The colour is so inviting and the texture is super creamy. Although the pea flavour is the dominant one, you'll also sense a subtle hint of exotic coconut, which provides a nice twist. I love serving this soup with a drizzle of olive oil and homemade croutons (yum!).

This pea soup made it to the list of my favourites because of very special memories it holds.

My dad loved peas. He would always have them on his plate at dinner time whether he was having a steak or roast chicken. I thought of him as a pea connoisseur because he had a special way of cooking peas and would never allow anyone else to cook them. I found it annoying when he would tell me off, but now I would give anything to have my dad tell me to leave the peas for him to cook. I miss him so much!

It's such mundane moments that enrich our existence, and food is the messenger of these beautiful memories.

Ingredients

1/2 bunch of fresh coriander, roughly chopped
200g peas, frozen
2 large spring onions
400ml coconut milk
A pinch of salt
A pinch of black pepper
1 tbsp #RESPECT

Method

Add the ingredients to a pot and bring to the boil.

Simmer for 5 minutes and then allow to rest for a couple of minutes.

Transfer to a blender and blend until smooth.

Pour into a bowl and EAT!

COOKING TIME 5 mins
FREEZER-FRIENDLY Yes
C, RSF, NF

SERVES 2

Glazed Miso Pumpkin

*Oh my Lord... this glazed pumpkin is beyond yummy
and it's twice as good the next day on toast.*

*Yeah, you read that right – mashed miso glazed pumpkin on toast
is heavenly delicious. I love the combination of pumpkin sweetness
covered with a shiny and flavoursome miso glaze.*

*You know by now that I like to keep things simple,
and this recipe is yet another one that takes minimal effort to make.*

*There is one thing to be mindful of. All ovens are different, so you'll need to keep an eye
on yours and make sure the pumpkin doesn't burn. Before you start baking, make sure
you use a tray that will fit your pumpkin nicely. Also, the baking paper should go up the
sides of the tray so that it traps the miso marinade and won't let it leak onto the tray.*

*You are now all set and ready to make this fantastic dish. I love to serve it with a huge
bowl of salad topped with roasted, crunchy nuts and seeds.*

Ingredients

FOR THE MARINADE:

1/2 cup shiro miso paste
4 tbsp apple cider vinegar
1/2 cup maple syrup
4 tbsp coconut sugar
2 tsp chili flakes, optional

FOR THE PUMPKIN:

10 slices of pumpkin
(I used kabocha pumpkin)
1 tbsp #LETTINGGO

Method

Preheat your oven to 350F/175C. Line a baking tray
with baking paper and set aside.

TO PREPARE THE MARINADE:

Whisk together all the ingredients. Taste and adjust
the level of sweetness if needed.

TO PREPARE THE PUMPKIN:

Arrange the pumpkin wedges on the baking tray.

Pour the marinade over the pumpkin and coat the
wedges on both sides.

Bake in the preheated oven for 30 minutes.
Flip the wedges and continue baking for 30 more
minutes or until the pumpkin is cooked through.

When done, leave to rest and cool down a bit.

Serve over a bed of greens and enjoy!

PREP TIME 10 mins
BAKING TIME 50 mins
FREEZER-FRIENDLY No
C, RSF, NF

SERVES 4

Corn Chowder

*Lush, rich, and with a depth of flavour... that's how I like to describe this corn chowder.
My mates love it, especially when it's served with yummy garlic bread and a drizzle of
olive oil. It's such a wonderful meal that really allows corn to shine and show its glory.*

*The main advice I can give you to make sure that you nail this recipe is not to
blend the entire mixture. Just blend half because chowder is the best
when there is some texture in it. I love to add sliced spring onions and fresh
coriander and parsley as they complement the corn flavour really well.*

*Don't wait, make this beauty today and send loads of love to all our farmers
who work so damn hard to grow corn and allow us to enjoy such epic meals.*

Ingredients

2 tbsp coconut oil

4 corn cobs, kernels
removed

1 onion, finely diced

1 yellow capsicum,
finely diced

3-4 garlic cloves,
finely chopped

1/2 celery stalk,
finely diced

4 cups coconut milk

Salt and black pepper,
to taste

Fresh herbs, such as
parsley, coriander or spring
onions, for serving

1 tbsp #SELF-WORTH

Method

Heat a large pot on medium-high and drizzle in the
coconut oil.

Add the corn kernels, onion, capsicum, garlic, and celery
and season well with salt and pepper. Cook for 5 minutes,
stirring continuously.

Pour in the milk, scraping the pot base to pull the brown
bits off.

Put the lid on and bring to the boil.

Turn the heat to low, cook for 5 minutes and then transfer
half of the mixture to your blender.

Blend until creamy, and then return back to the pot.

Taste, adjust the seasoning if needed, pour in your serving
bowls, top with some chopped fresh herbs and enjoy!

PREP TIME 5 mins
COOKING TIME 5 mins
FREEZER-FRIENDLY No
C, RSF, NF

SERVES 2-3

Detox Mung Soup

This is an Ayurvedic, healing dish that your body will be grateful for. The earthy flavour which comes from the mung beans is lifted to a new dimension by a spice bomb that will spread intoxicating aromas all over your kitchen and make you feel like you are in India.

I love this recipe because I feel my body appreciates the care it gets through this soup, and it's ridiculously easy to make. You'll have to keep your eye on one thing, though. If you notice the water is evaporating fast and the spices are not strong enough, just add more (a little at the time).

It will be fine if you cook the soup on super low with the lid on.

To get the full experience, I'd like you to grab a chair, sit next to the stove while the soup is cooking, take a few deep breaths and properly receive the energy and care you are about to give to your body.

Ingredients

1 cup dried mung beans, soaked overnight in 500ml water
4 cups water
1/2 tsp hing or asafoetida
1-2 fresh green chilies, finely chopped (optional)
1 tsp cumin seeds
2 tsp coriander powder
1/2 tsp turmeric powder
1/3cm cinnamon stick
2-3 whole garlic cloves
8-10 fresh curry leaves, finely chopped
1 tbsp grated fresh ginger
1 tbsp lemon juice
1 tbsp coconut sugar
1 1/2 tsp salt, or to taste
A handful of fresh coriander, chopped
100ml #LOVE

Method

Drain the beans, rinse well and add them to a pot together with all the remaining ingredients.

Cook on low-medium with the lid on for about 45 minutes.

Top with the fresh coriander and enjoy!

SOAKING TIME overnight
COOKING TIME 45 mins
FREEZER-FRIENDLY Yes
C, RSF, NF

SERVES 3

Detox Carrot & Almond Soup

This is an epic cold soup! Although the list of ingredients is very short it's actually packed with a flavour that is enhanced by the salt. It's great as it is or served with chopped carrots, avocado, or capsicum. Some of my friends have it when they follow a detox menu but I enjoy it regularly, and sometimes even as a snack before dinner.

The thing I really love about this type of simple dish is that it amazes me over and over again with the fusion of flavours and isms they can create. When you serve this vibrantly orange beauty, let positive thoughts flood you and then say to yourself: I love my life!

Ingredients

300ml fresh carrot juice
1 shallot, roughly chopped
2 cups fresh almond milk
Salt and black pepper,
to taste
1 tbsp #TRUST

Method

Add the ingredients to your Vitamix and blend for at least a minute.

Pour into a bowl and treat yourself!

PREP TIME 5-10 mins
FREEZER-FRIENDLY Yes
R, RSF

MAKES 650ML

Broth

This broth will be your best friend if you decide to go on a juice fast. It's a great add-on to your juice menu, especially in the evening, as a perfect end for a long day. I found that it has a calming effect on me, grounds me into my body and gives me a warm hug from the inside out. Some of my friends enjoy it instead of a morning coffee and say that it puts them at ease.

When I'm fasting I take the veggies out of the broth and put them back into the soil in my garden. They act as a potent nourishment for my plants. On days when I'm not fasting I keep the veggies. They are so well cooked that even the tiniest cells in them decompose and release enormous amounts of flavour.

It freezes really well and you can use it when making risotto, soups, and stews as a flavour booster.

Ingredients

2 heads of broccoli, cut into big chunks

2-3 corn cobs, cut into big chunks

1-2 onions, roughly chopped

6 garlic cloves, smashed

2 large zucchinis, cut into big chunks

4 medium carrots, cut into big chunks

3 potatoes, cut into chunks

250g button mushrooms, whole

1-2 leeks, both white and green parts, cut into big chunks

2 celery sticks, roughly chopped

100g fresh parsley, roughly chopped

8L water

2 tbsp salt

1 tbsp black pepper

1 cup #EASE & FLOW

Method

Add all the ingredients to a large, 15L pot.

Bring to the boil, reduce the heat to low and cook for 3 hours.

Allow to rest before serving.

PREP TIME 10-12 mins
COOKING TIME 3 hours
FREEZER-FRIENDLY Yes
C, RSF, NF

MAKES 7L

Chocolate is life.

Hot Drinks

Forget everything you know about calories, vitamins, trace minerals and macro-nutrients.

Just drop that baggage right here. Mother Nature takes care of that. Pay attention to how good you feel when you eat real food. That's all you need to know.

Now kick back and enjoy a Hot Drink.

Lemon Ginger Tea

When I made this for the first time I loaded it with sweetener, drank half of it and kept half in the fridge. I reheated it later on and it still tasted amazing.

On a hot day I felt like drinking something cold so I tried this lemon and ginger tea with no sweetener and it was incredibly refreshing. Nothing hits the spot like a tall glass of my lemon and ginger ice tea on a scorching summer day.

And you know what the best part is? It's simple to make and is a much better option for your organs than store-bought teas, which are often packed with artificial flavours and loaded with sugar.

Do it for love. Do it for yourself. Do it for lemon and ginger ice tea.

Ingredients

250ml freshly squeezed lemon juice
2l water
150g ginger, smashed
Sweetener of your choice, for serving
1 tbsp #LOVE

Method

Add the ingredients to a pot and bring to the boil.

Let simmer for 30-40 minutes.

Strain, add as much sweetener as you like and enjoy!

Store in the fridge when cooled down in a bottle or jug with a tight lid. It stays fresh for a week.

COOKING TIME 30-40 mins
FREEZER-FRIENDLY No
C, RSF, NF

SERVES 4

Rosella Tea

This is one of my go-to drinks. Why? Well, the flavour is delicious and the colour shows me that whoever or whatever created us was super smart because the red colour is just magnificent.

Rosella makes for the best ice tea ever when cooled, loaded with ice and muddled slices of fresh oranges. Some of my mates take it to the next level by adding a big splash of vodka to the mix. Yeah, you know who you are. LOL.

Ingredients

550ml water
10g dried rosella flowers
Sweetener of choice, as much as you like
1 tsp #PEACE

Method

Fill a small pot with water, add the rosella flowers and sweetener and bring to the boil.

Turn down the heat and let simmer for 5 minutes.

Turn off the heat, let it steep, and then strain. Don't throw away the flowers. Toss them to your garden, back to the earth, allow the nature to break them down and return them back to the source. We sometimes rush around to buy ingredients and forget where they actually come from.

Pour into teacups and enjoy its relaxing fragrance and flavour.

PREP TIME 5-8 mins
FREEZER-FRIENDLY No
C, RSF, NF

SERVES 2

Orange Cinnamon & Star Anise

Infuse infuse infuse. That's all I have to say.

*Allow the flavours to do their dance with time
and your tastebuds will thank you later.*

Ingredients

1/2 orange, sliced
1 cinnamon stick
3 star anise
2 cups boiling water
1 cup #FAITH

Method

Add the ingredients to a teapot and cover them with 1 cup of boiling water. Let it sit for 30 minutes.

Pour in the remaining cup of boiling water, stir well and serve.

PREP TIME 30 mins
FREEZER-FRIENDLY No
C, RSF, NF

SERVES 2

Apple Cardamom Cinnamon Tea

*Being a non-tea-drinker I will confess I am no expert on the ways of the tea.
Growing up and living in a hot climate, cold drinks have been my go-to
for as long as I can remember, and tea used to be hot, flavoured water
that required sugar or milk to in order to bring it home.*

*I was first introduced to making tea without tea leaves,
milk or sugar in a health retreat I worked at over 15 years ago.
The team would gather after every evening meal, grab teapots and tiny cups,
slice up some fruit, put them into teapots together with spices and pour in boiling water.
This would sit until all the tables were cleared, and then they would top up the teapots
with boiling water and place them on the table for the guests to help themselves.*

*I tell you what, it was the highlight of each evening! Guests would ask where they could
buy the brand of the tea and were blown away after finding out how we made it.*

Now, back to this glorious apple tea infused with cardamom and cinnamon.

*There's something about how the fragrances of apples and cinnamon dance together.
To fully enjoy this tea, pour it into a tiny cup, go outside, sit on the ground,
take a deep breath and enjoy the intoxicating aroma.
Then sip away and appreciate the fact that epic tea doesn't
have to be made with dried leaves.*

*If you feel inspired to experiment with other fruit teas, go ahead!
Keep in mind that juicy and flavourful fruits work better for this type of tea.*

And don't boil it! Just let it steep.

Ingredients

1/2 apple, chopped into
8 pieces
2 cardamom pods,
smashed
1 cinnamon stick
550ml boiling water
1 cup #GRATITUDE

Method

Add the apple, cardamom, and cinnamon to a teapot and
pour in half of the boiling water. Let it sit for 30 minutes.

Top with the remaining boiling water and serve.

PREP TIME 30 mins
FREEZER-FRIENDLY No
C, RSF, NF

MAKES: 550 ML

Alkalise your thoughts. Alkalise your heart. Alkalise your gut.

Sweet Spiced Milk

This is an aromatic, hot and sweet milk that's quick to make with no fuss at all. It's my go-to sweet drink and it makes out like a little hug when there's no one else around. I'll brew up some spiced milk, curl up on the couch, snuggle into my blanket and sink into the love I have for my body and the gratitude I have for the life I've led so far.

I sip away, close my eyes and fall into the NOW as I hold myself knowing that I'm never alone. I have myself, and I'm so worth taking care of.

You'll feel the same when you take your time to brew this special concoction and sip it lovingly.

Ingredients

2 cardamom pods
1/2 tsp vanilla seeds
1 clove
2-3 dates, pitted
550ml coconut milk
A pinch of salt
1 cinnamon stick
1 tbsp #CARE

Method

Add everything except the cinnamon stick to a blender and blend until well combined.

Transfer to a pot, add the cinnamon stick and cook on low (don't allow the milk to boil).

When your spiced milk is hot enough, transfer to a cup and serve.

PREP TIME 1 min
COOKING TIME 5-8 mins
FREEZER-FRIENDLY No
C, RSF, NF

MAKES 550 ML

Cacao

If you are new to the idea of cacao paste, welcome to all its glory. What is it? It's the natural product of ground cacao nibs, which come from the fruit of the Theobroma cacao tree. Cacao paste (also called cacao liquor) is made by roasting the nibs lightly and crushing them into a liquid. This liquid quickly solidifies at room temperature and the result is glorious cacao paste. BOOM!

Now, what can I say about this cacao drink? It warms your soul with its chocolate fragrance holding hands with the sweetness of maple and the decadent creaminess of coconut milk.

Wrap yourself in a blanket and treat your soul with a mug of this amazing drink.

Ingredients

45g cacao paste
450ml coconut milk
Maple syrup,
as much as you like
A pinch of salt
1 tbsp #ACCEPTANCE

Method

Add everything to a blender and blend until well combined.

Transfer to a small pot, cook on low and keep stirring continuously to make sure it doesn't burn.

Serve hot.

PREP TIME 2 mins
COOKING TIME 8-10 mins
FREEZER-FRIENDLY No
C, RSF, NF

SERVES 2

I lead with 3 principles which form the foundation of my work: inspire, educate and transform.

Farming

*My dear friend Costa said to me years ago
We are all farmers
The consumer (You), the wholesaler, the retailer and the buyer are all farmers*

It was a statement which made total sense to me. I have spent time with farmers. I have harvested food. I have prepared that food. And of course I have eaten that food.

Like everyone else I've also spent enormous amounts of time buying food.

We are all connected with the farming process, whether it's through our hands, our hearts or our wallets. But most of us have lost touch with the actual process of farming. Many of us don't know whether pineapples grow on trees (they don't), where cashews come from (trees), or the many delicious varieties of tomatoes
out there.

When a farmer plants a seed he has worked extremely hard to create the right conditions for that seed to succeed. If he's an indigenous farmer like my friends from PNG and Bali, or any farmer with a long connection to the land, he will have access to knowledge from his tribe and community as well.

The rhythm and harmony of farming is truly an expression of nature, and this vast intelligence is also part of us as individuals and a species.

However, with modern distribution methods, the products of farming are delivered to us from all over the globe and we are disconnected from the work, care and effort involved to get it to our table.

We've become used to eating food grown in distant lands, far removed from its source, and usually grown with farming practises which deplete soil and reduce nutrients.

It's for these reasons and many more that I'm a fierce supporter of traditional, organic and biodynamic methods of farming. Growing food according to the rhythm and intelligence of nature means soil quality is preserved, nutrients are retained, the practise is sustainable, and the local community is supported.

I feel good when I use my wallet to vote for this style of farming food. And I feel good when I prepare and eat food from these sources. My heart sings knowing I am supporting communities and businesses and farming methods which work as closely with nature as possible.

And I love meeting the farmers themselves!

Most of us have no idea what goes on in one 18 hour day of farming. But I'm deeply grateful that farmers do. And in turn I'm deeply grateful to buy and receive such amazing food. I get to prepare meals with reverence that support my body and nourish my organs, my heart, my soul, and my community.

And I'm also deeply grateful that you are a part of my community. That I get to share with you the fruits of my labour, and show you how I care for the soil of my body and my mind, just like any good farmer will do.

Soil is the soul of everything.

Recipes

Acknowledgements

Mum. For reminding me to eat the many colours of veggies. For allowing me to venture as a child outside home to the back of Dad's workshop and amongst the locals on their kitchen floors who taught me how to make food from scratch. I love you!

Jayman. My son. For your constant push for better textures and flavours. You're a fan of your Mother and you're also the only person in my life that tells me if it's not good enough. Your words are brutal. It sometimes hurts, but always in a good way. I love you.

My brother BJ. Because you still have me in stitches as you take the piss out of all that I do. I love you.

My dear friends Valerie and Andrew. For the many creations, dinners and laughs we've had over the past 20 years. The countless recipes we prepared, celebrated and experienced as a family were born from the cooking shows and cookbooks we loved. We've had some spectacular cook ups over years which led me to the chef I am today. Forever grateful for your friendship.

Kat Dawes. Where do I begin? How about right NOW. I am undeniably a better version of myself due to your friendship and coaching. You're the most forgiving person I know. You have held my hand through heartbreaks and heart surgery. I am forever grateful for your unconditional love, your guidance and your willingness to cook. I love you so much.

Christina I adore you, I absolutely love how you can create a give back model in your business when there is a crisis around you. Your swift thinking and leadership in your life spills over into your business. I admire your creativity, strength and your brilliance. And I love how much you love tahini.

My beautiful and caring girlfriend Rachelle, the fussiest eater I know. I don't know anyone else that will plan a week's worth of meals like you. When you find something you love, you run with it for days. I love that about you and too many other things to name.

To the teams and the chefs in my world who have risen to my challenge to BE and cook from a place of love and respect for nature. I honour you. Thank you for allowing me to lead you.

Donna. One of the most active cooks I know. You're a creative genius in the garden and your studio and you create screen prints and designs which I adore. You have been by my side through my darkest moments and have kicked my butt when I was in my ego. I treasure your guidance and care over the years.

Hayley. Thank you for sending me so many recipes to create and make better. Your belief in me is humbling.

Paula. Your love of my work over the past 17 years has truly impacted my life. I love you dearly.

Simone. My dear, dear friend and co-creator of cafes we have built over the years. Thank you for your calm in my storms. How the hell you put up with me I don't know. Thank you for believing in me. Every time I've announced in a panic "I can't do that" you reply "yeah you can mate" and we continue on. You taught me how to see the solution even when I don't want to. I love how you have such little interest in impressing anyone as you quietly tinker in the background on your own, taking apart things and putting them back together in even more beautiful ways. You're an endless perfectionist and you bring order to my chaos. I love how you love my food.

Daina. My dear friend. You have impacted my life in rich ways that have connected me more to my body than ever before. Thank you for your genius and for the past year sitting on my studio table while we endlessly discuss human behaviour and the body . I treasure those moments sipping tea and eating chocolates seasoned with salt till the wee hours of the morning.

My BFF and #goddaughter of glory Seaenah. You have the audacity to taste my food and say yuck and loves me anyway. #littlegenius

Carl. You're a marketing genius. You bring a positive vibe to our many meetings we have each week and your ability to see my work not only though your clever brain and eyes but taste buds is humbling. Thank you for being on this ride with me. Your belief in my work is most welcomed. We have a lot to do my friend. Alot.

Russ. The Great Writer Man. It was my dream many years ago to work with you and now look at what we've done. I honour your creativity and truthful writing genius. Also that thread you created for my friends to record their favourite quotes by me was #genius. Unfortunately most of them aren't fit to be published lol. We'll just have to write another book huh.

Dee Thank you for your sharp eye and the positive vibe you bring to my world.

Brendalyn. My Mary Poppins. You came into my life when I needed all the business support, love and care. Forever grateful for your constant supervision (you know I need it), your smart mind and the love of food.

Gun Gun. Your calm, precious energy behind the camera captures my dishes effortlessly. For over eight years we've been eating, taking photos and filming together. You taught me how to stop when I watch you lay down a mat or a piece of wood and prepare to pray. I am forever grateful for our friendship.

Kymba. Our first call was to map out my brand and explore what is possible online. I still remember it to this day. Your guidance over the past eight years has been incredible. Your ability to design not only this book but all my creatives has been life-changing. I am forever grateful for your time and brilliance you bring to my heart and mind.

Jon. How did I manage to get Jon Gwyther – Director extraordinary brilliant mind, incredible cinematographer and photographer to say yes to helping me with my book? Let's just say Allllll My friends are jealous. I am forever grateful for how you extract the truth that I hide at times. How you gracefully and at times painfully allow that beautiful truth to tell its own story through a lens you hold. You are a genius. And I am honoured to call you my mate.

To you the reader for spending your hard earned cash on me. You have contributed to my rent!! THANK YOU. I trust you are in a place that is filled with hope, a chance to start again, to see the brilliance in new Beginnings and to be gentle with your journey. And to please remind yourself that you really do matter and your worth taking care of.

Chef Cynthia Louise xx

About Chef Cynthia Louise

Chef Cynthia Louise talks about food.

Plant-based food that makes you Feel GOOD.

She won't talk diet.

She won't talk macronutrients.

She talks about real food. Just like nature intended.

And one more thing – if it doesn't have flavour it can F-off.

Chef Cynthia comes with a large side of personality. An infectious passion. Not to mention she's also

- the bestselling author of 7 recipe books (including 3 books with biochemist Dr Libby Weaver)

- the star of 2 cooking shows on Gaia TV and FMTV

- the partner of a global chain of restaurants with serial entrepreneur Roger Hamilton

- served hundreds of people on stage and at retreats in Bali with Tyler Tolman

- and created her own range of gut-healing food products and online classes.

She's an exciting and charismatic public speaker touring Australia for the past decade. Thousands of people who live healthy, pain free, abundant lives through her meals say she knows what she's doing – and it works.

In her early days at a health resort she saw the effects of her cooking on chronically ill patients.

Diabetes, stress, chronic fatigue, Crohn's, eczema, cirrhosis, leaky gut, IBS and autoimmune conditions all responded positively – even to the amazement of natural doctors and

healers – when she served natural, plant-based meals made from her highest intentions.

She followed these same principles while recovering from her second heart surgery. So she knows the power of her method from the inside out.

As an adopted child raised in New Guinea, Cynthia spent days down the back of her family's workshop with the wives of the workers. They would harvest coconuts and shred them while roasting sweet potatoes over an open fire. In contrast, her nights at home were spent eating rissoles and mash (don't ask what a rissole is if you don't know).

She learnt early on how real food tastes and what it does for your body.

That's when she realized that cooking is a contract with your body. Our health is on loan. You pay it back by nourishing yourself with positive energy and emotions, then starting the simple act of preparing a meal.

It's one of the many simple, yet profound things Chef Cynthia Louise has discovered in her journey. And there's more she wants to share.

Cook with real food. Cook with great energy. Cook with Chef Cynthia Louise.

Continue the Love Story

For a glorious flow of plant-based recipes, videos, hints, tips and online classes, follow me on:

@ chef cynthia louise   www.chefcynthialouise.com

Cover design and layout by Kymba Burrows

Food Photography by Gun Gun Gumilar

Photography by Anna Bek

Photography and direction by Jon Gwyther

Food styling by Chef Cynthia Louise

Recipes by Chef Cynthia Louise

All props provided by Chef Cynthia Louise studio kitchen

Author Plant-based Love Stories Chef Cynthia Louise

© Chef Cynthia Louise 2020

Publisher Let's EAT Food

First printed in 2020

ISBN: 978-0-6450178-0-9

IMPORTANT NOTE TO READERS: Although every effort has been made to ensure all contents of this book is accurate, it must not be treated as a substitute for qualified medical advice. Always consult a qualified medical practitioner. Neither the author nor the publisher can be held responsible for any loss or claim arising out of the use, or misuse of the suggestions made or the failure to take professional medical advice.

Lightning Source UK Ltd.
Milton Keynes UK
UKHW051131191021
392416UK00002B/157